Globalism and Regionalism
Jonathon Porritt

black dog publishing
london uk

THE EDGE
FUTURES

By the year 2025 the climate will have changed irrevocably, mainly as a result of greenhouse gas emissions. The temperature is predicted to be, on average, half a degree warmer and will fluctuate to a greater extent. Rainfall will have reduced but will also become more extreme. Resources such as energy, water and food imports will be in shorter supply and transport will be constrained; partly as a result of climate change but also due to regulations aimed at preventing global warming. In this series of important and timely books the Edge explore the impact these changes will have on our lives in the future. Global in scope and far reaching in its implications this series examines the significant social, environmental, political, economic and professional challenges that we face in the years ahead.

Contents

Foreword
Chris Twinn

In the West we have become dependent on globalism to deliver prosperity and the vantage point from which we now feel able to consider environmental sustainability. Yet that same globalism is viewed as largely responsible for exceeding the carrying capacity of our planet in terms of natural resource extraction and waste absorption.

According to the United Nations the stabilising of worldwide population growth, which may provide the only chance of living within our planet's resource, follows from the harnessing of lower labour costs in developing regions and providing them with some local prosperity.

At present it is the lack of local prosperity that fuels those minorities who wish to disrupt world stability and with it any managed process focused on the objective of all people having a right to a fair share the world's natural resources.

But widening access to prosperity through globalisation is increasing competition between countries. Those with the highest growth rates and largest economies are already buying up future finite natural resource availability through strategic alliances and by playing political hardball. Those who lose out will be those we have not yet developed sufficiently to acquire the influence for a piece of the world resource cake as it is now carved up between the major players. Their frustration at seeing the door to prosperity closed in their face we ignore at our peril.

Globalism and Regionalism considers the impact that dwindling resources and restricted travel will have on global competitiveness and regional identity. Competition between countries is likely to increase. Whilst this may lead to conflict, it could also facilitate greater creativity. This in turn will put a premium on technological advancement and on an ability to respond rapidly to change. Simultaneously, regionalism possibly based on city regions rather than nation states, will develop and localities could become more distinctive and potentially aggressive.

Those already on the growth ladder have their development path mapped out for them courtesy of developed countries. They will seek to pass as quickly as they can from their industrialisation phase, through a service economy phase to become a highly lucrative creative economy. China is already aware that its labour cost basis is rising and is focusing on completing this progression in perhaps a tenth of the time the United Kingdom has taken. By investmenting in some 250,000 engineering graduates a year their rapid progression in this regard looks highly likely.

Already there are signs that the era of very cheap imported consumer products upon which the developed world's recent prosperity growth has been based is beginning to pass. Easy access to very large quantities of fossil energy is being curtailed by both limits on supply and much higher levels of demand. With uncertainty of supply will go price instability as major world events repeatedly trigger availability concerns. How much of our current prosperity growth rate will we be prepared to sacrifice for more expensive world goods and services?

In the meantime, a new regionalism is likely to develop, based on city regions rather than nation states. The local approach allows a more proactive political leadership in response to local sustainability concerns and is better able to manage the cyclical use of resources in a supply-constrained world. This contrasts with the historical linear process with its hidden resource extraction and final waste disposal, all dealt with by remote parties in remote locations.

At present such new regionalism is somewhat simplistic in believing that it can make significant improvement in isolation. Indeed the growing tendency to put a red line around regional targets ignores the fact that the poor performance of others is a direct result of our impacts, witness the goods made for us in China.

A move to regionalism should not ignore the fact that a significant part of our Ecofootprint will remain remote and part of the global system. It might seem attractive to seek a Medieval town arrangement, fed directly by its countryside hinterland, in return for providing back a proportion of local prosperity. We can no doubt make better use of local resource for more of our needs. But our lifestyle expectations have moved on and our ability to produce all we need locally is unrealistic. It may well be less carbon intensive to transport biomass from Scandinavia for running our buildings, than truck it the length of the UK. Indeed, a ship also offers more opportunity for being powered by renewables in the future than a lorry. Our Ecofootprint could be distributed anywhere across the world as long as we are reducing our demand (together with its delivery) to our fair share of bio-productive planet area.

Getting our own house in order is an essential starting point. This is where regionalism can really help, particularly in the developed world where we have more economic scope to explore options for a less resource intensive lifestyle. This process, which is currently preoccupied with technical fixes, is likely to demonstrate that technologies might be enablers in this process, but it is the individuals and their decisions that determine the direction of our overall environmental impact. UK energy building regulations have been with us for more than 30 years, but energy use per household continues to rise, despite there now being fewer of us in each household. For although we have more sophisticated heating systems, we now heat every room to allow the kids to use their computers in their bedrooms, instead of heating one room where all the family gathered. We are now used to temperatures that allow us to wear shirts sleeves in winter where once we wore pullovers and quilted waistcoats!

We are entering a world where carbon labelling of products, buildings and services will be the norm and will inform a local agenda of economy and restraint. But the regional message will also feed into education and the global transfer of ideas to provide ideas, products and lifestyles for the wider world.

Introduction
Jonathon Porritt

There is something incredibly tired about today's debates on globalisation. It is as if all the music critics of the 1970s and 80s were still laying claim to pre-eminent roles in critiquing contemporary music: one respects their longevity, but their acuity—let alone their relevance—leaves a lot to be desired. The world has changed so much in the last 20 years— physically and geo-politically, not metaphorically—as to make much of the theorising on the future of globalisation somewhat laughable.

There are two things in particular. As the world has got richer, year on year, as measured by the standard metrics of increasing economic activity, so has it got more inequitable.

According to the 2004 report of the "Commission on the Social Impacts of Globalisation", nearly two in three of today's 6.5 billion people live in countries where the gaps between the richest and the poorest are getting wider, not narrower—60 years of astonishing economic productivity leaving the world a less just rather than more just place in which to live.

The idea that constantly widening equity gaps are somehow compatible with any serious understanding of a "sustainable economy" is so puerile as to beggar belief. If that sentence offends you, then pick up an elastic band, stretch it, stretch it further, question fleetingly whether it can really be stretched anymore, stretch it some more, and see what happens. After all, history is littered with spent elastic bands.

And then try climate change. Climate change changes everything in the way you see the world, or you simply haven't seen climate change for what it is. Which, unfortunately, was the case for the vast majority of government delegations who gathered together in Bali, in December 2007, and failed utterly, to come up with a response to climate Change commensurate with the incredibly robust scientific consensus that now exists.

So I wonder how Bali will be remembered in the annals of climate change diplomacy? A "good beginning" as Ban Ki-Moon put it, conveniently forgetting that this was exactly how the 1992 United Nations Framework Convention on climate change was described, and exactly how the Kyoto Protocol was subsequently described as well.

A "tawdry, ineffective compromise", as I heard one Non-Government Organisation (NGO) representative describe it, bitterly aware of the fact that what was being compromised, yet again, was the integrity of the life support systems on which we all depend.

My favourite, at this stage, is "the final shaming of America". Al Gore's words, not mine, uttered in despair at the implacable intransigence of the Bush administration's negotiators, offered with his right arm stretched over his chest as if he was standing in front of the American flag, as if seeking some inner strength in order to say such 'unpatriotic' things.

But thank God a few Americans are actually saying them. I spent quite a bit of this year reading books about the role of America in a post-9/11 world—including John Gray's *Black Mass: Apocalyptic Religion and the Death of Utopia*, and most recently, Naomi Kline's astonishing *Shock Doctrine*. It numbs the mind to have to come to terms with the utterly hateful force and reach of today's United States imperium, a truly 'evil empire' if ever there was one.

To have so comprehensively lost America as an international 'force for good', at a time when the world needs more than ever that kind of energy and generosity of spirit that America brought to bear on post-war Europe in the twentieth century, has to be just about the most depressing aspect of a world that has, quite literally, gone to war on itself.

The image of The Last Chance Saloon inevitably comes to mind. But Bali did at least agree on a two year deadline for establishing a successor to the Kyoto Protocol. The US Presidential election is in full swing, and all of the candidates, in both parties, have adopted much more progressive positions on climate change—and on the role of the US in the world today—than the current incumbent. Americans themselves want dramatic change on both counts and oil has just gone through the symbolic $100 a barrel threshold— paradoxically, probably the best thing that could happen in the short term, from a climate change perspective, with the huge knock-on benefits it will bring in terms of energy efficiency, technological innovation, renewables and so on.

But not such a good thing from the equity perspective, as the biggest impacts of high-priced energy will be, as ever, on the world's poorer countries. And this kind of dilemma (the need for very high fossil fuel prices as a foundation for any serious strategy for a low-carbon economy, balanced against the need to dramatically reduce rather than reinforce those economic disadvantages that are keeping many poor countries in such dire poverty, precisely encapsulates the need to totally rethink today's largely irrelevant debate about the future of globalisation.

Climate—proofing Globalisation

I have this enduring memory of the launch on 30 October 2006 in London of the Treasury-sponsored report by Sir Nicholas Stern, "The Economics of Climate Change". There is the man himself, looking a little startled at the media hubbub, doing his best to live up to his reputation as "a dry as dust economist", as some newspapers described him the day after. There was Tony Blair, the Prime Minister at that time, radiating the kind of intent, nervous energy that the combination of climate change and high-profile media moments always brought out in him. And there was Gordon Brown, Prime Minister-in-waiting, more observer than participant, looking unsure as to whether or not he should have been there at all.

The combination of speeches delivered on that day should have changed politics in the UK dramatically, immediately and irreversibly. The weight of scientific analysis, the unhesitating acceptance of the need for urgent action, the recognition that the UK, having assumed a unique leadership role in pursuing international solutions to climate change, had to commit first and fast in its own back yard, and the remorseless logic of Sir Nicholas Stern's economic calculus, left everyone who had come with an open mind (there were, of course, a few journalists present whose professional lives depend on the absence of any such faculty) in no doubt that they were witnessing the demise of anything vaguely resembling economic 'business-as-usual'.

> The investment that takes place in the next ten to 20 years will have a profound effect on the climate in the second half of this century and in the next. If we don't act, the overall costs and risks of climate change will be equivalent to losing at least five per cent of global Gross Domestic Product (GDP) each year, now and forever. If a wider range of risks and impacts is taken into account, the estimates of damage could rise to 20 per cent of GDP or more. In contrast, the costs of action—reducing greenhouse gas emissions to avoid the worst impacts of climate change—can be limited to around one per cent of global GDP each year.[1]

1 Stern, Nicholas, "The Economics of Climate Change": The Stern Review, Cambridge: Cambridge University Press, 2006

One year on, The Stern Review is more talked about in China and the US than it is here in the UK. The Treasury has done an exceptional job spinning its own report as a major contribution to the international debate, but of only limited relevance to policy-making here in the UK. Nicholas Stern himself has left the Treasury, and plunged back into academic life at the London School of Economics—as well as acting as an adviser to HSBC and to the Chinese government as it prepares its own look-alike report. The truth of it is that even the most rigorous economic logic must still bend the knee in the face of 'political reality'. That reality is bounded by the laws of international competitiveness and "first-mover disadvantage" which means that any one nation state (or even a trading block as big as the European Union) is likely to be penalised in the short-term for unilaterally internalising the cost of a particular environmental externality (in this case, the costs associated with continuing to emit very high volumes of CO_2 and other greenhouse gases into the atmosphere), whilst everyone else stands by and enjoys their windfall advantage. But Nicholas Stern's *Review* is crystal clear on what he calls the "balance of risks":

> If the science is wrong and we invest one per cent of GDP in reducing emissions for a few decades, then the main outcome is that we will have more technologies with real value for energy security, other types of risk and other types of pollution. However, if we do not invest the one per cent and the science is right, then it is likely to be impossible to undo the severe damages that will follow. The argument that we should focus investment on other things, such as human capital, to increase growth and make the world more resilient to climate change, is not convincing because of these irreversibilities and the scale and nature of the impact.[2]

2 Stern, "The Economics of Climate Change"

His overarching conclusion ("that the world does not need to choose between averting climate change and promoting growth and development") is one that underpins the core thinking behind this particular treatment of globalisation and regionalism. Indeed, I would be tempted to paraphrase and extend Nicholas Stern's conclusion as follows: "the world does not need to choose between learning to live sustainably on Planet Earth and promoting environmentally sustainable growth and socially inclusive development—just as long as we get on with it in the very near future". If we don't get on with it in the very near future, the world will indeed have to choose between the two—or, rather, will have that choice imposed upon it as the iron-clad laws of Nature trump the vainglorious and massively over-hyped laws of the Market.

This urgency is precisely what makes a growing number of commentators so apprehensive when the Intergovernmental Panel on Climate Change (IPCC) informs its political masters that they have no more than "ten to 15 years" to put in place the policy platforms from which a genuinely low-carbon global economy will eventually emerge. Ten to 15 years! What's more, that's the consensus view of a body which has been widely portrayed since the publication of its *Fourth Assessment Report* in 2007 as an immensely conservative body, working as it has to on the basis of finding near-total consensus amongst its contributing scientists, and then having to persuade member countries (including the US, China, India, Saudi Arabia and so on) to sign off on every single word. There are few scientists who genuinely believe that the 'scientific snapshot' captured in the *Fourth Assessment Report* properly reflects the state of the science as they see it today.

In an extraordinary article published in the *Philosophical Transactions of the Royal Society* in June 2007, James Hansen (Director of NASA's Goddard Institute for Space Studies) and a number of colleagues pointed to the likelihood of a much grimmer outcome before the end of this century:

> Recent greenhouse gas emissions have placed the Earth perilously close to dramatic climate change that could run out of control, with great dangers for humans and other creatures. The IPPC analyses and projections do not well account for the non-linear physics of ice sheet disintegration, ice streams and eroding ice shelves, nor are they consistent with the palaeoclimate evidence we have presented.[3]

3 Hansen, James, "Climate Catastrophe", *New Scientist*, 28 July 2007

The evidence they are referring to relates to ice cores taken from both the Arctic and the Antarctic ice sheets going back over 650,000 years. These ice cores have revealed a number of instances where sea levels have risen by several metres in less than a century—for example, about 14,000 years ago, sea levels rose by approximately 20 metres in 400 years, or about one metre every 20 years. What this means, according to James Hansen, is that the IPPC's projection of a sea level rise this century of somewhere between 18 to 59 cm is, in all likelihood, a massive underestimate, and that a rise of "several metres" is the much more likely outcome of the current level of man-made emissions.

It is that almost unmanageable continuum of views (a few centimetres vs. a few metres) that will I hope explain why I am making such a big deal about climate change in a text about globalisation and regionalism. Climate change is the first indisputably global phenomenon, affecting the totality of natural systems and habitats that make up the biosphere. Even ozone depletion (which loomed very large indeed as an international problem back in the 1980s) was not strictly 'global' in its impacts and effects, and even environmental disasters such as the continuing destruction of the world's rainforests (which will indeed have devastating global consequences) are regional in their primary impacts. The only global environmental problem that runs climate change close is the inexorable build up in the environment of toxic, persistent and bio-accumulative chemicals, traces of which (and sometimes very substantial traces) can be detected in every single square metre of the Earth, including the most inaccessible mountain peaks, deserts and 'wilderness' areas.

Climate change is also the first indisputably global political phenomenon in that it is literally impossible to address the potentially catastrophic consequences of "runaway, irreversible climate change" without every single nation on Earth being party to the necessary remedial measures. The reality of non-negotiable interdependence is one that most world leaders (particularly in the US, China and India) currently seek either to avoid or simply cannot comprehend, imprisoned as they are in their nationalistic fortresses.

But there is no denying that reality. As the receiving medium, the atmosphere works as one unified system, with absolutely no dividing lines, incapable of distinguishing between a molecule of CO_2 emitted in Beijing or in Bognor Regis or in Bogota. By the same token, contribution and consequence are not proportionate: the impacts of climate change on the US and Africa, for instance, will not be in proportion to the scale of their own emissions, resulting in what will come to be seen over the next few years as the most grotesque global inequity we have ever witnessed, with countries that have contributed next to nothing to the overall problem suffering an intolerable burden, whilst those who have contributed massively scramble to adapt by engineering their way out of the worst consequences— albeit at massive cost, but with some temporary prospect of reduced impact.

The science of climate change demands either that we come rapidly to that point of globally recognised interdependence, or that the awareness of this interdependence dawns on people far too late, so that we end up sliding inexorably into a world where doing anything globally (other than via remnant internet communities) will become all but impossible over the course of the next 100 years or so. In evolutionary terms (as far as our own tiny little splinter of reconstituted DNA is concerned), what we're looking at here is a battle of competing tipping points so vast in scale that it makes Malcolm Gladwell's treatment of said tipping points look insignificant.

On the one hand, we have James Hansen's ultimate tipping point: the point at which our species loses the ability to command its own destiny. It doesn't necessarily lose the ability to survive (in that the human species is startlingly adaptable and resilient, and could easily 'hang on in' over thousands of years in fragmented micro-communities, even in the teeth of catastrophic, non-linear climate change), but it will have little say about the terms on which we survive. Modern 'civilisation', as the rather precarious jewel in the crown of human endeavour over many millennia, will become an anthropological artefact, nostalgically investigated by imperilled academics tired of grubbing around in their subsistence allotments.

On the other hand, we might just arrive at that shared, globally-recognised sense of interdependence before we slide off miserably into civilisation-crushing climate change. And in so doing, as I shall further explore, we might just set the world on an infinitely more secure and equitable path than the one we are blindly stumbling down at the moment.

That is our excruciatingly painful and 'right now' reality. Yet it is remarkable just how little the reality of climate change has as yet impacted on the debate about globalisation. For all sorts of reasons, these two huge, continent-spanning agendas, two policy super-highways running parallel to each other, with thousands of government officials, NGOs, and academics streaming down each of them, rarely if ever intersect.

The final months of 2007 entail critical milestones for both processes: the Conference of the Parties (under the United Nations Convention on Climate Change) in Bali in December 2007, and the final throes of the international negotiations to bring the Doha Round on trade liberalisation to fruition before the end of the year. But each is all but blind to the other, as if government negotiators were already finding things so difficult in their own specific area of concern that they dare not risk further diversions by widening the boundary conditions. Even more surprisingly, this blinkered approach on the part of governments is almost entirely duplicated in NGO positions—so much so that I find most of the campaigning literature about Doha and the threats of contemporary globalisation incredibly anachronistic. This is a debate that has followed reassuringly polarised tramlines since the mid-1990s and particularly since the "anti-globalisation movement's" defining moment on the streets of Seattle in November 1999—but it is now way off the pace when it comes to internalising the implications of accelerated climate change.

For the time being at least, world trade talks are still deemed to be much more important than global environmental processes, including the convention on biological diversity, measures to restrict the spread of toxic chemicals or halt the abuses of over-fishing, as well as climate change. The World Trade Organisation occupies a dominant position in the architecture of today's international order, with powers of sanction and a dispute settlement mechanism that allows it to ride roughshod over all other UN bodies—it is, *de facto*, the closest thing we have to world government today. And in the eyes of many, it represents the absolute antithesis of the kind of global governance we will need in a resource-constrained world.

Global Futures

However, with 2025 in mind, rather
than 2008, I have therefore decided not
to reprise the historical debate about
the pros and cons of contemporary
globalisation—and having sought to
do justice to that particular debate
in *Capitalism as if the World Matters*,
I hope it's not inappropriate to refer
readers to that particular source if that's
their principal area of concern. What
matters more for the purposes of this
text is to identify some of the different
scenarios it is possible to tease out
of the current debate (however firmly
and conservatively fixed in its historical
tramlines it may be) as to the likely
'state of globalisation' over the next
15 to 20 years.

There are, in essence, just four:

1. **Globalisation As Is**
2. **Globalisation Transformed**
3. **Globalisation Reborn**
4. **Globalisation In Retreat**

Globalisation As Is

This is the dominant view of those primarily in government and business, and in the World Trade Organisation (WTO) itself. They tend to see globalisation as "an unstoppable force impacting on every square inch of the world today". Even the potential collapse of the Doha Round has not dimmed the enthusiasm of those who are prepared to acknowledge some of the 'downsides' of globalisation, but are convinced (more often than not in good faith) that the 'upsides' massively outweigh the downsides. Certain limited reforms are happily countenanced (in the operations of the WTO, for instance), but 'if it ain't broke, why fix it?' mindsets remain firmly in the ascendancy. This 'official' position commands powerful endorsement from an extremely impressive line-up of mainstream economists and pundits from Jagdish Bhagwati, Johan Norberg and Martin Wolf, whose *Why Globalisation Works*, 2004, provides a most compelling account both of the benign impacts of globalisation and its future potential. As far as the mainstream media are concerned (such as *The Economist* and *The Financial Times*), that seems quite sufficient. Everything else is just irrelevant froth.

Globalisation Transformed

It is not sufficient, however, for a number of very influential 'insiders' who have seen for themselves just how defective the current model really is. The most eloquent exponent of transformation rather than incremental reform is undoubtedly Joseph Stiglitz, former Chief Economist

to the World Bank, whose double-barrelled assault
on contemporary globalisation (*Globalisation and its
Discontents*, 2002 and *Making Globalisation Work*, 2006)
systematically dismantles the very institutions which would
seek to control any reform agenda.

Stiglitz and like-minded 'insider critics' have come up with
a set of far more radical prescriptions. But (and it is a big
but), theirs is a scenario still based on massively increased
trade, rip-roaring economic growth, few restrictions on
capital markets, and only marginally extended regulatory
controls on the operational freedom of multinationals.
Transformation of a kind, but not of the system as a whole.

Globalisation Reborn

Leading lights in the "anti-globalisation movement" (as
it is incorrectly described) have always been at pains to
point out that there are few movements more global than
theirs, and that the real debate is about power, control
and democratic accountability—not about globalisation
per se. A leading group of campaigners came together
in the run up to the World Summit on Sustainable
Development in Johannesburg in 2002 to produce the so-
called "Johannesburg Manifesto", based on the following
distinction between two starkly differentiated models of
globalisation:

> Broadly speaking, there are currently two concepts of
> globalisation which have gained prominence in recent
> controversies. Corporate globalisation, which aims at
> transforming the world into a single economic arena,
> allows corporations to compete freed from constraints
> in order to increase global wealth and welfare. This
> particular concept can be traced to the rise of the free
> trade idea in eighteenth century Britain and has come,
> after many permutations, to dominate world politics in
> the late twentieth century.

Democratic globalisation, on the other hand, envisages a world that is home to a flourishing plurality of cultures, and that recognises the fundamental rights for every world citizen. The roots of this concept extend back to the late ancient Greek philosophy and the European Enlightenment, with their perception of the world in a cosmopolitan spirit. We believe that the cause of justice and sustainability would be caught in quicksand unless it is elaborated upon in the framework of democratic globalisation.[4]

4 "Johannesburg Manifesto", *Fairness in a Fragile World*, Berlin: Heinrich Böll Foundation, 2002

In other words, economic growth and increased trade are not ends in themselves, but potentially useful means to achieving much broader objectives at the heart of which lies the ideal of social justice.

Globalisation in Retreat
One of the intellectual glories of 40 years of passionate debate about the environment is a school of thought that sees conventional economic growth as the principal source of the problems we face today, and the globalisation of that economic paradigm as the single most pernicious driver of social injustice and environmental destruction. Increased trade in and of itself, is therefore an abomination, and the machinery of global government (as vested in the International Finance Corporation (IFC), the World Bank and the World Trade Organisation) is characterised as an unaccountably successful means of enslaving the vast majority of the world's people in order to enrich an already inconceivably rich elite.

There is a robustness and uncompromising integrity about this particular strain of anti-globalisation that one cannot fail to admire. But the alternative it proposes (in terms of what might be described as "double devolution", with power reverting first to the nation

state and then down to the local community) remains
frankly unappealing to most people, and is often
contemptuous of humankind's material aspirations. Self-
sufficiency may well become a rallying cry after the kind
of economic and social collapse that many now see as
entirely unavoidable, but I still believe it has very little
traction as a means of warding off that collapse.

So how do these different scenarios fare in terms
of successfully internalising the twin imperatives
of sustainable development, namely "living within
environmental limits" and "securing a world based on
social justice and democratic accountability"? Against a
somewhat crude scoring matrix, with a low of one and a
high of five, here's how I would assess them:

Scenario	Environmental Limits	Social Justice
Globalisation As Is	1	1
Globalisation Transformed	3	3
Globalisation Reborn	4	5
Globalisation In Retreat	5	2

I shall come back to the relationship between these very
different globalisation scenarios and the prospects for a
resurgence of regionalism in "Rediscovering the Regions".
But first, it seems crucial to determine some of the key
parameters of what life will actually look like in 2025, in
terms of what we know almost for certain, what we can
be reasonably confident about predicting, and what still
remains highly speculative.

2025—for better or for worse

Anyone asked to provide a snapshot of the world 20 years or so from where we are now will inevitably feel somewhat humbled by the Rumsfeld Continuum, based on some original work by Michael Lacey:

> As we know, there are the known knowns. These are the things we know we know. We also know that there are known unknowns. That is to say, we know there are some things we do not know. But there are also unknown unknowns—the ones we don't know we don't know.
>
> Donald Rumsfeld

Moving from the 'knowns' all the way through to the 'unknown unknowns', many of the predictions being made today depend entirely on what one believes about the speed with which today's dominant paradigm of progress through exponential economic growth will start to erode or even implode. Our starting point here has to be the combination of population and climate change.

Population
We can, in fact, be reasonably confident about the number of human beings with whom we will be sharing the planet in 2025—around 8.25 billion, up by around 1.8 billion from today's population of 6.4 billion.

Elsewhere, I have written extensively of the bizarre conspiracy of silence that renders otherwise intelligent and compassionate people mute in the face of today's demographic realities. Almost without exception, progressive environmental, social justice and human rights organisations have persuaded themselves that the increase in human numbers is of itself an irrelevance to their principal concerns. The dangers of this systematic self-delusion were stripped bare in a 2006 report from the UK's All Party Parliamentary Group on Population ("Return of the Population Growth Factor") which concluded very simply as follows: "the evidence is overwhelming: the Millennium Development Goals are difficult or impossible to achieve with the current levels of population growth in the least developed countries and regions".[5]

5 "The Return of the Population Growth Factor", All Party Parliamentary Group on Population, Development and Reproductive Health, January 2006

As it happens, the Millennium Development Goals are not particularly strong on environmental concerns, but it is already self-evidently the case that the impacts of climate change and increased human development (see below) can only be exacerbated by the arrival in our midst of another 80 million or so people every year:

Millennium Development Goals
Goal 1: Eradicate extreme poverty and hunger
Goal 2: Achieve universal primary education
Goal 3: Promote gender equality and empower women
Goal 4: Reduce child mortality
Goal 5: Improve maternal health
Goal 6: Combat HIV/AIDS, malaria and other diseases
Goal 7: Ensure environmental sustainability
Goal 8: Develop a Global Partnership for Development

The 50 poorest countries in the world will more than double in size, from 0.8 billion in 2007 to 1.7 billion in 2050, according to UN projections published in March 2007. Increases in population of this scale and rapidity will wipe out gains in agriculture, education, literacy or health care faster than they can be made. Alleviation of poverty by even moderate increases in per person wealth, however justified, will have major impacts on climate in the environment because of the sheer numbers involved.[6]

Climate Change

Concentrations of CO_2 in the atmosphere are currently at around 384 parts per million (ppm). They are increasing at around 2.2 ppm per annum, and this figure itself inches upwards every year as countries like China and India ratchet up their own emissions—by the end of 2007, China became the single biggest emitter of CO_2 in the world.

6 Guillebaud, J, *Youthquake: Population, Fertility and Environment in the 21st Century,* Optimum Population Trust, 2007

By 2025, concentrations will therefore be at around 420/425 ppm, based on the assumption that the first phase of the Kyoto Protocol (which ends in 2012) has delivered only nugatory reductions, and that the second phase (assuming that there is a second phase!) will have begun to deliver some serious reductions in the second half of the decade. (This is all calculated just on CO_2, by the way, so such projections do not allow for other greenhouse gases such as methane, nitrogen oxide and so on.)

The new consensus around climate change is a simple and strong one: our primary objective has to be to ensure that average temperatures do not increase by more than 2°C by the end of this century. The IPPC tells us that we have already seen at least a 0.7°C warming up to 2000, and that there is at least another 0.5°C—0.6°C already "in the system"— taking account of the lag time between the point of emissions released into the atmosphere and their full warming effect. And that same consensus then goes one step further: that means emissions of CO_2 should not exceed more than 450 ppm if we are to stay below that 2°C threshold.

That much is reasonably clear, but given that humankind has never actually cooked a planet before now, scientists are reluctant to go hard and fast on just how 'perturbed' the climate is likely to be by 2025. They do understandably remind politicians (and all those sapheads in the media who believe that there are going to be as many upsides from climate change as downsides) that everything we are witnessing today by way of extreme weather events is a consequence of the CO_2 and other greenhouse gases we put into the atmosphere more than 20 years ago—the same 'lag-effect' referred to above.

Suffice it to say that the economic and social impacts could already be horrendous by 2025—even if we're well into our CO_2 reduction curves by that stage. That's the conclusion the world's insurance industry came to some time ago. In January 2007, the Chairman of Lloyds of London, Lord Levene, calmly informed the World Affairs Council in Washington that "the insurance industry today faces the prospect of a $100 billion national disaster— roughly twice the scale of Hurricane Katrina. We need to wake up to the truth about catastrophe and radically review our public policy." (That's polite business speak, by the way, for "get your finger out and stop dithering around".) The re-insurance industry (which picked up 80 per cent of the $50 billion bill from Hurricane Katrina) has been in no doubt about the rising curves of climate-induced natural disasters, and privately believes that the total damages bill could double every decade—to bring that down to earth, that translates into a totally new bottom line in the global economy within the next 50 years, with insurance losses from climate-induced disasters equalling in any one year the total value of GDP in the global economy.

Eco-system Pressures
Every other year, World Wildlife Fund (WWF) produces its *Living Planet Report*, highlighting the net impact of the human economy on the natural world. It's an extraordinary document, aggregating detailed data from biomes and eco-systems all around the world in a process that is not dissimilar to that of the IPCC as it relates to climate change. The principal measures it uses are "the Ecological Footprint" (which shows the extent of human demand on eco-systems around the world) and the "Living Planet Index" which basically monitors the health and resilience of those eco-systems in terms of biodiversity. The 2006 *Report* summed it all up as follows:

Since the late 1980s, we have been in overshoot.
The Ecological Footprint has exceeded the Earth's
biocapacity—as of 2003—by about 25 per cent.
Effectively, the Earth's regenerative capacity can no
longer keep up with demand—people are turning
resources into waste faster than nature can turn
waste back into resources.

Humanity is no longer living off nature's interest, but
drawing down its capital. This growing pressure on eco-
systems is causing habitat destruction or degradation
and permanent loss of productivity, threatening both
biodiversity and human well-being.

For how long will this be possible? A moderate business-
as-usual scenario, based on United Nations projections
showing slow, steady growth of economies and
populations, suggests that by mid-century, humanity's
demand on nature will be twice the biosphere's productive
capacity. At this level of ecological deficit, exhaustion of
ecological assets and large-scale ecosystem collapse
becomes increasingly likely.[7]

7 WWF, *Living
Planet Report*,
WWF International,
Switzerland, 2006

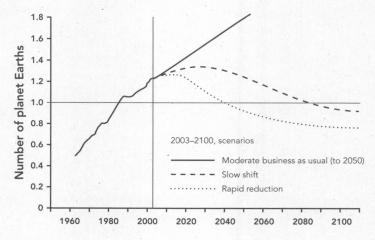

People tend to think of this 'biodiversity crunch' as being of little importance in comparison to something like climate change. But I urge you to draw your own conclusions from this, bearing in mind that there has been no serious rebuttal of any of the data in these Living Planet Reports. Indeed, the principal response from governments, bodies like the World Bank and the World Trade Organisation and global business organisations, has been silence. How, after all, can they possibly cope with data of this kind? Even a system as de-natured as ours still retains some residual, almost atavistic folk-memory that our human economy is still 100 per cent dependent on the healthy functioning of natural systems. But we have to excavate this suppressed knowledge from the deeper recesses of our collective mind in order to build it, explicitly and consistently, into every aspect of our modern lives.

Resources
When the original "Limits to Growth" report was published by the Club of Rome back in the 1970s, it gave birth to what has been an active and influential industry ever since then: the cornucopians. It is their collective task to rebut any suggestion that resources might be finite, or that there are clear physical and biological limits to the scale and reach of human economic endeavour. The cornucopians can look back on 30 years of outstanding achievement, having so successfully sustained some of the core myths of modern industrial society (for instance, that exponential economic growth is available to us indefinitely over time, that the laws of the market will seamlessly sort out any resource shortages, and that technological innovation will continue to deliver a world of cost free plenty for ever greater numbers of increasingly voracious consumers) that most world leaders today remain blissfully unaware of our unyielding physical reality: namely, that a combination of imminent resource shortages and looming

environmental limits will turn their aspirational dreams of constantly rising material plenty into a nightmare of thwarted expectations, economic dislocation and resource conflict. In short, the laws of thermodynamics have not been superseded by the laws of the Market—they have just been temporarily obscured by them.

So what do we actually know about future resource constraints—just so this is not seen as yet more recycled eco-propaganda from the 1970s. Scientists at Yale University published an interesting paper in the *Proceedings of the National Academy of Sciences* in 2006 looking at the production and consumption of key metals and concluded "virgin stocks of several metals appear inadequate to sustain the modern 'developed world' quality of life for all of Earth's people under contemporary technology".[8] This is particularly worrying as regards metals like tantalum (an essential component in the manufacture of mobile phones, and one of the key causes of the Civil Wars in the Democratic Republic of the Congo—which has the biggest tantalum mines in the world—between 1997 and 2002), platinum (a vital component not only in catalytic converters but in many different fuel cell prototypes—a technology on which the world may come to depend heavily in its search for more sustainable forms of transportation and power generation), indium (widely used to create the semi-conducting materials on which some of today's most exciting solar technologies depend), and so on.

8 *New Scientist,* 26 May 2007

Serious discussion as to the medium-term availability of key metals and minerals is rare—at least there was a proper debate about these things back in the 1970s! But two things are changing that. The first are the investments currently being made by the Chinese government in an extremely wide range of metals and minerals, particularly across the continent of Africa. This has prompted increased attention from the US Pentagon and security services in terms of long-term threats to US national security. The US Geological Survey recently revealed that the US is already importing more than 90 per cent of certain 'rare earth' metals from China, raising a serious question mark over future security of supply.

Second, the debate around the medium-term availability of oil is now back in the news big time. Notwithstanding the bland reassurances from the major oil and gas companies that there are no serious constraints on supply through until 2030, there is growing concern that a combination of factors (soaring demand in China and India, diminishing reserves of 'easy' or conventional oil, worsening security issues in places like the Middle East and Nigeria, and so on) could not only keep oil prices pretty high (it got pretty close to that $100 threshold on a number of occasions in the final quarter of 2007), but take them much higher. Even the International Energy Agency acknowledges that oil prices will never go back to where they were even a decade ago.

In one respect, it has to be said, this simply demonstrates that the laws of supply and demand are in good heart: as prices rise, new technologies and extraction techniques become 'economic', companies get more efficient in their use of oil, new reserves are brought in, demand falls, and pressure on supply diminishes. This is true—but that should not obscure the unavoidable reality that the so-called "peak oil moment" (the point at which we are half way through total oil reserves) cannot now be far away, and from that point on, the economic consequences of demand constantly exceeding supply will be felt throughout the global economy—and most particularly in those poor countries that would benefit most from access to relatively cheap fossil fuels to underpin their own development trajectories.

The size of the global economy

If this was a more conventional treatment of globalisation, there would now follow a swathe of variably euphoric projections as to the total size of the global economy, the speed with which it will double or even triple, the relative standing in a global league table of the US, China, Europe, India and other super powers, impacts on national GDP and on per capita income, and so on.

These projections are widely available, and mostly moonshine as far as I am concerned—inasmuch as they are nothing more than very crude extrapolations from where we are today and from what has happened in the past. The various matters raised in the four sections above have had no bearing on the way in which these projections are developed, as if we lived in two entirely disconnected worlds: the world of hard-edged empirical data regarding the flows of matter and energy through natural systems (including the human economy), and the world according to academic economists absorbed in their econometric models. Only very rarely—as in Nicholas Stern's "The Economics of Climate Change"—are these two worlds forced into one integrated framework.

But even this cursory examination of 'the state of the world' in 20 years time surfaces one incontrovertible reality about the future of the global economy: the poor are not going to be able to escape from poverty by a process of 'catch-up development'. Today's rich nations got rich primarily because of the easy availability of fossil fuels and because of 'empty' continents into which they could expand and commandeer plentiful raw materials. This 'bonfire of resources' simply cannot be repeated. As Wolfgang Sachs puts it:

The strategists of catching-up development, who still occupy the commanding positions in economics and politics, are prone to a tragic confusion: they think that in the twenty-first century it is still possible to succeed with the Utopias of the nineteenth. In reality, quite apart from the likely harm it will cause, an economic advance today has to face resource limits that are incompatible with the traditional models of production and consumption. The democratization of resource-intensive prosperity runs up against the economically or ecologically insurmountable limits of scarcity.[9]

The persistent and totally perverse refusal to re-orient today's debate about globalisation around these fundamental resource issues is all the more startling as security forces the world over are certainly alert to the looming chaos ahead. In 2003, the Pentagon published an extraordinary report on *An Abrupt Climate Change Scenario and its implications for US National Security*. Its conclusions make even the most dystopian warnings from Friends of the Earth sound positively upbeat, and it concluded with the sobering words:

As global and local carrying capacities are reduced, tensions could mount around the world, leading to two fundamental strategies: defensive and offensive. Nations with the resources to do so may build virtual fortresses around their countries, preserving resources for themselves. Less fortunate nations, especially those with ancient enmities with their neighbours, may initiate struggles for access to food, clean water or energy. Unlikely alliances could be formed, as defence priorities shift and the goal is resources for survival rather than religion, ideology or national honour.[10]

9 Sachs, W and T, Santarius, *Fair Future: Resource Conflicts, Security and Global Justice*, London and New York: Zed Books, 2005

10 US Defence Department, "An Abrupt Climate Change Scenario and It's Implications for US Natural Security", quoted in *Black Mass*, 2003

As others have since pointed out, that risk is further compounded by the possibility that resource wars will converge with wars of religion—ensuring that some people's worst fears about a potential "clash of civilisations" becomes self-fulfilling. This is certainly the view of John Gray, whose devastating *Black Mass: Apocalyptic Religion and the Death of Utopia* pours scorn on the kind of position adopted in this paper. Just because the world is more interdependent than in the past,

> that is no reason for thinking that it is going to become more co-operative. Where states remain strong and effective they will act to secure the resources under their control. Where states are weak or collapsed, the struggle will devolve to other groups. The overall result is intensified conflict rather than global co-operation.[11]

11 Gray, J, *Black Mass: Apocalyptic Religion and the Death of Utopia,* London: Allen Lane, 2007

So where does that leave the case for a renewed emphasis on regionalism?

Rediscovering the Regions

Ours has undoubtedly been the Age of the Global. Over the last 25 years, 'big picture politics' has reflected an overwhelming preoccupation with all things global. Literally thousands of books and academic papers on various aspects of globalisation have emerged; the nation state is widely perceived to have been 'in retreat', with decisions shaped more and more by the over-arching challenge of prospering in a global economy. The 'unstoppable force' of globalisation has impacted not just on every square inch of the world today, but on every political process, every last aspect of governance, every constitutional development.

Even in those countries where the constitutional balance between national government on the one hand and the provincial, state or regional levels of government on the other, remains both healthy and dynamic, the encroachment of global imperatives has indeed proved to be all but unstoppable.

This is certainly the case in Europe. The driving force behind the rapid expansion of the EU has been to create a 'global player' which in terms of scale (population) and strength (economic power) will be able to compete successfully with the US, China, India and the Far East. That has to be dressed up in all sorts of different ways, but that is what Europe is now all about. The new EU Constitution remains loyal to some of the old ideas that brought European nations together (a desire to avoid further wars, to create a 'level playing field' between member countries, an affirmation of the value of cultural exchange and so on), but is basically about just one thing: promoting competitiveness in the global economy.

The old but still very attractive idea of a 'Europe of the Regions' has been severely eroded by the Lisbon Agenda: competitiveness in the global economy demands the subjugation of regional, local and community interests to the 'greater good' of achieving economic success in the global economy. That compelling hierarchy has emerged in our lives almost by default, in that politicians are reluctant to spell it out in such a way that voters would clearly understand that the global must now trump not just local and regional perspectives, but national perspectives as well. Under Scenarios 1 and 2 in "Global Futures" ("Globalisation As Is" and "Globalisation Transformed"), that hierarchy would remain firmly entrenched. It is sobering to see the relative ease with which the globalisation/liberalisation faction within the EU Commission, clustering around different aspects of the Lisbon Agenda, have been able to outmanoeuvre a rather larger (but less influential) number of Commissioners who represent in their own countries an agenda much closer to that of the Gothenburg Process: social inclusion, maintenance of key rights and entitlements for workers and citizens, better environmental protection and so on. The language of Gothenburg may still be omnipresent, but it is the iron fist of the Lisbon Agenda that shapes EU policy today.

The resulting 'fudge' (that globalisation and regionalism can happily co-exist and indeed are mutually reinforcing) is now standard fare for voters across the whole of Europe. The deterministic assumptions that lie behind this implicit hierarchy (that the nations of Europe 'have no choice' in that we either learn to prosper in the global economy or prepare for penury, and that long-term gain—however nebulously articulated—will compensate for any short-term pain) are usually only questioned for very different reasons either by Europe's right-wing populist parties, concerned as they are about national sovereignty and about the erosion of cultural identity in the face of mass immigration, or by Europe's Green Parties, who see our subservient acquiescence in the so-called 'economic imperatives' of globalisation as the greatest accelerator of environmental devastation and social injustice.

It is time that those wanting a fairer, more environmentally sustainable world, where everyone's basic needs are met, had a radical rethink. They must stop pinning their hopes of campaign success on tweaking the direction of globalisation. They must stop acting as if trade rules were governed by some kind of Olympian logic that comes down from on high, with the intention of eventual global benefit. They must set their campaigning ambitions higher than differential adjustments to the onward march of globalisation. Instead, trade rules should be seen for what they are: a grubby set of global guidelines drawn up at the behest of the powerful for the benefit of the powerful.[12]

12 Hines, C, *Localisation: A Global Manifesto*, London: Earthscan, 2000

Only under Scenario 3 ("Globalisation Reborn") will a concept of "A Europe of the Regions" really flourish. Cultural, economic and political heterogeneity would be the norm and highly prized; individual citizens would be encouraged to see themselves as part of a bigger region (Europe as a whole), but their primary "identity relationships" would be with their own particular region (the North East of England, Bavaria, the Basque Country, Emilia Romagna, the Peloponnese and so on) and with their local community. In an interesting pamphlet for the new Local Government Network, Ed Balls, John Healey and Chris Leslie emphasise the crucial importance of this issue:

> The question of identity is vital to creating sustaining structures of governance, because it goes to the heart of how we as a society co-exist. All individuals strive for security, comfort and a sense of belonging in their lives. Our identity is inextricably linked with those we interact with, and the normal patterns of social behaviour through which we live our lives. Good governance works within the framework of our social psychology. Matching our political institutions and discourses with our social and personally constructed identities helps to anchor them positively within society.[13]

13 Balls, E, J, Healey and C, Leslie, *Evolution and.Devolution in England*, New Local Government Network, 2006

It is still uncertain, mind you, just how enthused this Labour government really is about further radical steps to devolve power through the English Regions and on to local government. There is an ambivalence there that still muddies the water in every new stuttering measure it advances to regulate the relationship between the centre and the local. By contrast, decentralisation (down to the regional, local or community level) has always been 'an article of faith' for green activists the world over. The rationale behind this rests on four thematic pillars: economic, democratic, cultural and ecological.

Economic

The watchword here is self-reliance: produce as much locally and regionally as it is possible to do, efficiently and cost-effectively, and buy in whatever else is needed from as close to home as possible. This is not the same as self-sufficiency, a cause which has always attracted a small but influential number of advocates arguing that there should be few if any exceptions to the prioritisation of local production for local needs. I shall revisit this crucial distinction, in the final chapter, as part of a wider exploration of what a genuinely sustainable balance between globalisation and regionalism might look like. But in a carbon-constrained world, with energy and commodity prices rising ever higher, it obviously makes sense to reduce the length of supply chains wherever possible—though this has huge ramifications for the global economy as we know it today.

Democratic

Green Parties have always subscribed enthusiastically to that school of thought which believes that a thriving democracy is built from the bottom up and not imposed from the top down. As concerns about declining participation in elections grow—particularly at the local level—the correlation between the level at which decisions are being taken and the degree of engagement/ detachment on the part of the individual citizen regarding such decisions becomes more and more important. Whether the traditional 'rule of thumb' in green thinking (that all decisions should be taken as closely as possible to those most directly affected by them—or "radical subsidiarity" as it is sometimes called) still commands the same level of support in today's globalised world is a moot point: many individuals feel little if any direct involvement in their local community, often opting instead for engagement in a variety of virtual (and increasingly global) communities through the internet.

Cultural

Diversity of every description remains a significant issue for green activists the world over. One of the central concerns in today's multifarious campaigns against globalisation is the damage it is perceived to do to cultural diversity through the 'homogenisation' of economic and cultural activity, as well as through the concentration of power in the hands of fewer and fewer global companies. The right to protect cultural diversity from the forces of globalisation has for some become as important as the fight to protect biological diversity. A world dominated by American values and lifestyles, transmitted ever more persuasively by the vast and powerful US entertainment industry, has become an increasingly abhorrent prospect as people take stock of the incalculable damage done by the imposition of America's imperialistic ambitions all around the world. Critics of globalisation like the Indian academic and activist Vandana Shiva point out that we cannot really separate cultural diversity and biological diversity anyway:

> Diversity is the characteristic of nature, and the basis of ecological stability. Diverse ecosystems give rise to diverse life forms and diverse cultures. The co-evolution of culture, life forms and habitats has conserved the biological diversity of the planet. Cultural diversity and biological diversity therefore go hand in hand.[14]

14 Shrybman, S, *A Citizen's Guide to the World Trade Organisation*, Ottawa: Canadian Center for Policy Alternatives, 1999

Ecological

Anthropology reveals the cumulative overlay of human culture on the workings of the natural world over many centuries, reaching out further and further into parts of the world once deemed inaccessible, and deeper and deeper into the complex relationships and interconnections which underpin the healthy functioning of those natural systems.

Such insights have often simulated a much more
creative approach to regionalism than is apparent in
our mainstream media today. Throughout the 1970s
and 80s, a philosophical/political movement known
as "bioregionalism" played an extremely influential
role in elaborating green thinking, particularly in the
US. For various reasons, that bioregional perspective
has been somewhat overshadowed of late, both by
increasingly hostile political developments at the
national level, and by the shift of emphasis to the
global—and not just the global economy—in terms of
global environmental issues such as ozone depletion
and now climate change.

However, as I shall explain in the next chapter, my instinct
is that the ideas underpinning bioregionalism will gain
new momentum over the next couple of decades, so it
is worth unpacking briefly what it means. In essence, the
original region is of course the biological region: any part
of the Earth's surface whose boundaries are more or less
determined by natural features and characteristics rather
than by any subsequent human overlay, distinguishable
from other regions by particular attributes of flora, fauna,
water conditions, micro-climate, soils and geological
features. The essence of bioregionalism as a political
movement is the overarching need to find ways of
working "in partnership" with these natural attributes,
rather than seeking to impose on them a standardised
industrial culture in order to squeeze as much economic
value out of them as possible—to become, in rather
more poetic discourse, 'dwellers in our own land' rather
than acting as invasive aliens. This is how Kirkpatrick Sale
summed it up back in 1991:

> To become dwellers in the land, to come to know
> the Earth fully and honestly, the crucial task is to
> understand place, the immediate specific place

where we live. The kinds of soils and rocks under our feet; the source of the waters we drink; the meaning of the different kinds of wind; the common insects, birds, mammals, plants and trees; the particular cycles of the seasons; the times to plant and harvest and forage—these are the things that are necessary to know. The limits of its resources; the carrying capacities of its lands and waters; the places where it must not be stressed; the places where its bounties can best be developed; the treasures it holds and the treasures it withholds—these are the things that must be understood.[15]

15 Sale, K, *Dwellers in the Land*, Philadelphia: New Society Publishers, 1991

That may sound a bit dated today, or perhaps a little too florid for the more pragmatic style of environmental thinking that seems to dominate contemporary political discourse. Interestingly, however, it is precisely the kind of philosophical approach that can be detected at the heart of the most important EU directives (the Habitats Directive and the Water Framework Directive) that will regulate our interaction with the natural world across Europe in increasingly influential ways over the next few decades.

Is a better world still available?

Critics of today's model of globalisation are often accused of having nothing to put in its place. In their new book, *Break Through*, Ted Nordhaus and Michael Shellenberger, ask why it is that environmentalists are only too happy to share with the world an endless litany of nightmarish dystopias, but somehow can't get themselves into any kind of "I have a dream" creative space:

> Martin Luther King Jr's "I have a dream" speech is famous because it put forward an inspiring, positive vision that carried a critique of the current movement within it. Imagine how history would have turned out had King given an "I have a nightmare" speech instead.[16]

16 Nordhaus, T and M, Shellenberger, *Break Through: From the Death of Environmentalism to the Politics of Possibility*, Boston: Houghton Mifflin, 2007

This is more than a little mischievous! In writing
Capitalism as if the World Matters, I had the opportunity
to review many different positive visions put forward by
environmentalists over the years, and had little difficulty
coming up with a composited version to encourage
at least some visualisation of how things might be
(see Appendix).

But the tension between centralisation and decentralisation
is ever-present in terms of alternatives to the current world
order. Any enquiry into the balance between that which is
best done globally and that which is best done regionally
(or locally) depends to a very large extent on what sort
of serious room for manoeuvre one believes there still
is for the future of humankind. For a variety of reasons
(predominantly ecological or political), many people now
believe this is a somewhat irrelevant enquiry, in that our
'destiny' as a species is already determined by what we
have done (or failed to do) over the last 50 years or more.

They may be right. Every year that we postpone requisite
measures to address climate change, for instance,
the greater the likelihood that the 'too little, too late'
persuasion will be proved right. Jim Lovelock, perhaps
the world's most eminent independent scientist, is
convinced it is already too late, even if we were to do
more than anyone today can even begin to imagine.
James Hansen, whose gloomy prognostications I referred
to earlier, would be loath to fall in with Jim Lovelock's
'too late' hypothesis, but represents nonetheless a
growing cohort of world class scientists who believe that
the 'too late' threshold is not so far away.

There is an intriguing paradox here: might it not be,
against all the odds, the unprecedented global calamity
of climate change that summons forth an equally
unprecedented level of global collaboration? To take that

one step further, would it ever be possible, without the threat of runaway climate change, to fashion a half-way decent, reasonably equitable, broadly sustainable way of life for the vast majority of humankind over the course of the next few decades?

The vast majority of environmentalists take a predominantly negative (or 'realistic', in their words) position on any such speculation. However, a thriving school of latter-day ecotopians would have us believe it will indeed be possible to fashion that kind of future, and it's not hard to get swept up in their uplifting enthusiasm. James Martin's *The Meaning of the 21st Century* exemplifies this school of thought here in the UK. Unlike those fashionable 'contrarians' such as Bjorn Lomborg (who steadfastly argue that there is no "ecological crisis", with or without climate change, and certainly no crisis arising out of the inequitable distribution of wealth and resources), James Martin's analysis of the state of the world today is as realistic and uncompromising as that of Jim Lovelock's—or, I believe my own. But his passion for new technology takes him so far out into a world of benign, apparently foreseeable and manageable technofixes, as to leave my head spinning!

Most challengingly of all, this technological cornucopia becomes the means by which today's most intractable, non-ecological 'train crashes" (as he himself describes them) are also best addressed. Unfeasibly wide (and still widening) divides between rich and poor are to be eased if not entirely resolved by quantum breakthroughs in technologies like human enhancement or nanotechnology; religious fundamentalism or extreme ethnic or racist hatred becomes somehow more manageable in a world where extreme-bandwidth telecommunications based on fibre-optic cables with

inconceivably large transmission capacities make for
a globally connected world such as we have never
seen before.

Unlike many of my colleagues in today's increasingly
diverse Green Movement, I find myself moderately
susceptible to these technology-driven escape
routes. For instance, I have become passionate about
Concentrated Solar Power (CSP)—a simple, already
proven, more-or-less economically viable technology
(even in today's grotesquely distorted energy markets)
which would permit today's most generously solar-
enabled nations (some of which just happen to be
amongst the world's poorest nations) to generate far
more energy over the next 20 or 30 years than would be
required by the whole of humankind. This is not so 'over
the top' as you might suppose. It comes as a surprise
to many people to discover that investment in CSP is
already rising exponentially, with new and ever-larger
projects under way in more than a dozen countries—
even if, somewhat bafflingly, not one of the big oil and
gas companies has as yet staked a claim in what will
indisputably become one of the biggest global energy
technologies ever seen. Not even those companies with
an historical interest in solar power (particularly BP and
Shell) seem to have seen this particular inscription on
the wall.

Perhaps more controversially, my mind is also not entirely
closed to the prospect that the next generation of
nuclear power (as in the prototype pebble-bed nuclear
reactors being pioneered by countries such as China
and South Africa) might just come to the aid of those
already industrialised counties that still cannot quite see
their own particular future in terms of the decentralised,
small-scale, totally renewable technologies that our
collective future really depends on. It's just that my every

instinct about nuclear power tells me that until such time
as its inherent disadvantages (cost, unmanageable volumes
of waste, security risks, proliferation risks and so on) are
resolved, it is just pie-in-the-sky to suppose that nuclear
power has anything much to offer an imminently imperilled
human race. And as for nuclear fusion, you might as well
believe in Father Christmas.

All in all, you would have to be a congenital pessimist to
ignore the fact that the technology pluses in the world of
energy undoubtedly outweigh the technology minuses. That
is not the case in all spheres of human activity, and I will return
to the other main foundation of human life—namely food
production—in the next chapter. But that being the case with
energy, at least, there is absolutely no a priori reason why
governments should not already be single-mindedly driving
the transition from today's suicidally unsustainable fossil fuel
economy to a predominantly solar, renewable and increasingly
sustainable energy economy. There will, of course, be losers
in that transition (most spectacularly in those nations that
would otherwise have looked forward to drawing down the
trillions of dollars worth of fossil fuel assets that must now be
left exactly where they are in the ground), but as far as the
global economy is concerned, let alone nation states, let alone
individual citizens, Nicholas Stern's powerful arguments that
the costs involved in this transition will be relatively low (in
comparison to the costs involved in not making that transition)
must surely win the day.

But will it? Having ascertained that it is not technology
that is the problem, one has to look then either to the
capacity of political leaders and/or to the 'amenability'
of those who elect today's political leaders. And here the
prognostications are far from good. 50 years or more of
what George Soros describes as the "feel-good society"
throughout the developed world, but most aggressively
experienced in the US, has left the vast majority of people

today singularly ill-equipped to cope with an impending combination of dramatic change, much higher levels of societal and personal risk, and a renewed imperative for each and every citizen to 'play their part' just as would once have happened as a matter of course in less 'feel-good' periods of history. This is of particular significance in the US, which has been shielded from reality of almost every kind, seduced in the first instance by the delights of debt-driven consumerism and relatively low taxes, and, since 9/11, by the deception that all that is being asked of America as the sole superpower in the world today is to prosecute with increasingly ferocity a 'war on terror' that can obviously never be won.

> The message is simple: America cannot remain powerful and prosperous as a feel-good society. We must learn to confront unpleasant realities if we want to remain leaders in the world. Will any politician in the US stand up and deliver that message? And if there is such a politician, will the public listen? After all, a feel-good society does not want to be given bad news.[17]

17 Soros, G, *The Age of Fallability: The Consequences of the War on Terror*, London: Phoenix Books, 2006

I will return to the question of America and its role in the world in "Globalisation as American Imperialism". But for now, the only way of avoiding extreme pessimism is to assume that the increasingly painful reality of climate-induced 'shock and awe', combined with unprecedented levels of geo-political instability, will stimulate a different quality of political leadership, made possible and then reinforced by a different quality of citizen engagement. In *The Upside of Down*, Thomas Homer-Dixon draws a fine but critical distinction between breakdown, on the one hand (as in cumulative shocks to the system that still allow for full recovery and, eventually, for a fully-fledged 'breakthrough' to a better world), and, on the other, collapse—which allows for nothing other than a miserable descent into the end of any form of civilisation as we know it today.

For climate 'realists' (which is how scientists like Jim Hansen continue to see themselves), breakdown as a preamble to breakthrough is as close to optimism as one is permitted to come. Inevitably, it's a rather strange kind of optimism: for climate reality finally to dawn, globally and incontrovertibly in every nation, we basically need as much short-term pain in the system as it's possible to imagine. Not just one but, say, three Hurricane Katrinas every year over the next few years; not just 'weird stuff' in weather patterns in a few countries, but month-in, month-out extremes all around the world; not just 'a bit of a problem' for the world's insurance industry (which is how some in the industry continue to see climate change despite being in the eye of the financial storm that is now brewing), but partial meltdown in insurance markets all around the world.

Even this level of short-term pain will be horrendous. Growth in the global economy could slow and, for a while, even grind to a halt. But any residual scientific and economic doubts regarding the impact of climate change would be eliminated; electorates (and even those citizens living in non-democracies like China) would demand concerted, dramatic action on the part of their governments to ward off the prospect of much, much worse pain in the future.

This, at least, is the working hypothesis against which it is possible to assess what needs to be done at a global level and what needs to be done at a regional/local level. And in this regard, we're in for some very rude shocks to the unthinking assumptions of most politicians and economists today that volumes of globally-traded goods and services will simply continue to increase at more or less the same rates as they have done over the last 20 to 25 years. That simply is not going to happen as a combination of very high oil prices and serious measures to decarbonise the global economy finally kick in.

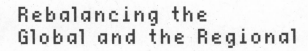

Rebalancing the Global and the Regional

Perhaps the most significant area of economic activity to investigate in that regard is agriculture. Few people today have fully understood the complex relationships between climate change and modern agriculture—which is both a major contributor to climate change and the one area of human endeavour most vulnerable to the impacts of accelerated climate change.

Depending on how you define the 'boundary conditions' around global food production systems, agriculture is responsible for anywhere between 15 to 20 per cent of global emissions of CO_2, 60 per cent of methane gas emissions, and up to 80 per cent of nitrous oxide emissions—a greenhouse gas that is at least 200 times more powerful than CO_2.

Emissions of nitrous oxide come from two principal sources: the conversion of forests into farmland, and the use of artificial fertiliser. Methane (which is around 20 times more powerful as a greenhouse gas than CO_2) arises predominantly from increased livestock production and from rice paddies—the hectarage of which has increased dramatically over the last 20 years.

Modern agriculture is, at one level, a massive success story. We would not have been able to increase human numbers as we have done without huge increases in agricultural production. Unfortunately, there are still many millions of people who do not have enough food to lead a decent life, but this is much more to do with lack of money than with any lack of food as such. For citizens of the rich world, on the other hand, food has become just another globally traded commodity. As long as the price is right, it matters not a fig to the food processing industry or to retailers where they source their raw materials from. Supply chains have become increasingly global, food prices have been kept astonishingly low throughout the rich world, and consumers have got used to (and, it has to be said, are delighted by) a vastly extended range of choices in which seasonality and country of origin are minor if not irrelevant considerations for the majority of consumers.

But these huge successes have only been made possible by the use of fossil fuels—in the production of nitrogen fertilizers and agricultural chemicals, in the development of ever more efficient farm machinery, in pumped irrigation, in sophisticated distribution systems and so on. The rapidly changing dynamics of energy costs, the availability of oil and gas, the growing impact of climate change policies, and the need to reduce the amount of water in modern farming (the amount of water used for irrigation is doubling every 20 years or so, and already accounts for around 70 per cent of the fresh water used world-wide) means this particular model of agriculture cannot possibly survive.

To take just one example, the over-arching need to ensure that the 1,600 billion tonnes of carbon locked up in soils all around the world stay locked up in those soils mandates a dramatic shift in farming practices—a challenge made all the more urgent given the latest work done by The Hadley Centre demonstrating that even gently rising temperatures over the next 30 years may well transform today's biggest 'sinks' for CO_2 (our forests, oceans and soils) into net CO_2 emitters. And whatever one may think about the potential for genetically modified crops, unless those new crops have built into their genetically engineered DNA attributes that massively reduce CO_2 intensity, from planting through to final use, then the contribution they will make will be of little value in a carbon-constrained world.

The simple reality is that, over the next ten to 20 years, our food economy will become predominantly local and regional, with much smaller volumes of international trade almost entirely in commodities such as tea, coffee, chocolate, exotic fruits, wine and so on—in other words, those 'special' products where mutual advantage may be said to justify a relatively greater carbon footprint. And most of these products will travel by sea rather than by plane, and will be Fair Trade rather than bog-standard. Food production systems will minimise the use of fossil fuels at every point in the value chain, and maximise the potential to sequester more carbon in both soils and biomass. There will be widespread use of manures, compost and mulches, such as forest bark, straw or other organic material; agro-forestry systems will thrive, and are in fact already being increasingly actively supported even by arch-promoters of modern intensive farming such as the UN Food and Agriculture Organisation.

Organic farming systems come closest to this model of sustainable agriculture at the moment, primarily because they avoid the use of all fertilisers and synthetic chemicals.

But we are unlikely to end up in an all-organic world by 2025, as the judicious use of artificial chemicals may well prove beneficial for the time being as part and parcel of integrated pest management systems. Organic or not, there will be far less meat consumed in the world, and the kind of feedlot-based systems of intensive meat production that we see today will become a thing of the past, symbols of old-world 'efficiency', where neither carbon nor cruelty played any part in the metrics used.

It has to be acknowledged that few people today feel much enthusiasm for this potential radical transformation in food production and distribution. All efforts to emphasise the importance of 'food security' in political debate today are still dismissed as an anachronistic default to pre-market protectionism. But the very idea of self-sufficiency in food production has been subtly corrupted, as pointed out by Teddy Goldsmith:

> The way International Agencies define 'self-sufficiency' has nothing to do with the way the term is normally used for a country that produces no food at all but can still be regarded as 'self-sufficient' so long as it can pay for its imports. What we call food self-sufficiency, they call 'food autarchy', and for them, this is the greatest crime any country can possible commit, for if it were adopted world-wide, there would be no international trade, no global economy, and no transnational corporations, while the economies of countries made dependent on world trade would have to be drastically transformed.[18]

18 Goldsmith, E, "How to Feed People under a Regime of Climate Change", *Ecologist Magazine*, January 2004

But advocates of local, self-reliant food production systems do themselves few favours by appearing to endorse, with more than a hint of nostalgia, the simplicities of traditional, 'peasant' subsistence farming. In fact, the only way the adoption of local food production systems will work (in developed countries, at least) is through increasingly sophisticated production techniques as well as distribution and marketing systems. 'Local' must come . to mean aspirational, higher quality rather than making do with 'what one has to put up with'. And one can easily imagine all the advantages of web-enabled, personalised systems, maintaining high levels of choice and diversity, becoming the standard in this very different food age.

This is important. If such developments are seen as a retreat from the high point of today's centralised and globalised systems, they will be resisted rather than embraced. The same is true of the next energy revolution, as societies move away from today's ludicrously wasteful, over-priced and carbon-intensive energy supply systems to a far greater reliance on decentralised energy technologies, local area networks, hyper-efficient homes, offices and shopping centres. To describe this as some kind of 'energy descent', a compulsory abnegation of all today's convenience and mindless plenty, is hardly going to make the politics of engineering such a transition any easier. The huge advantage of today's cutting-edge energy technologies (affecting both overall energy consumption and renewables) is that they're going to provide all our current energy services (or, at least, almost all—one suspects that the days of the patio heater are clearly numbered!) at little if any extra cost—and with massive sustainability benefits.

It is therefore with some confidence that one can point to at least two of the basic foundations of civilised life (energy and food) being as readily and satisfyingly available at a local/regional level as at a global/national level. Beyond that, there is also little reason to suppose that the same quality of life as we have today would not be maintained in terms of the provision of basic services such as healthcare, education, waste management, social services—these are already, after all, the primary provenance of local systems of governance, however much central government may seek to circumscribe levels of local autonomy.

In short, that which can be delivered locally and coordinated regionally, should be. The sustainability benefits (as in reduction of damaging environmental impacts) are substantial. But the idea that this somehow diminishes the importance of pursuing solutions to a host of other sustainability challenges at the global level strikes me as very bizarre. A strictly rational, function-based commitment to regionalism and localism does not need to be accompanied by some automatic ideological abhorrence of appropriate models of globalisation. Indeed, as already indicated in "Global Futures", the inherently global nature of challenges such as climate change, demand an unprecedented commitment to global institutions and processes without which no solutions can possibly be forthcoming.

And climate change must, of course, come at the top of that list—which means sorting out both China and the US! With China now the world's largest emitter of CO_2, overtaking the US in the second half of 2007, and the US still the world's most culpably deviant nation (in terms of ignoring its historical international responsibilities), any post-2012 successor to the Kyoto Protocol must explicitly start with the imperative of getting these two nations on board. Of the two, China is in fact the more important, in that the principal reason for the US refusing to ratify the Kyoto Protocol in the first instance was the fact that nations like China and India were not initially required to take their share of emission reductions. But once those countries are engaged, the rapidly shifting politics of climate change inside the US (especially in California, as well as in a growing number of big cities and key States) offers a more than reasonable prospect of the US coming on board. And on the China front, the global realpolitik is simple: there is a financial deal to be done, and it will not come cheap.

This is a wholly counter-intuitive position, but if one buys into the idea of "breakthrough via breakdown" (as articulated in "Is a better world still available"), it is not unreasonable to suppose that China will engineer its sustainability breakthrough long before the US or even Europe. China's understanding of climate-induced vulnerability (through further loss of productive land, depletion of water resources, sea level rises on its Eastern seaboard, social insurrection arising from disputes over land and water, and so on) runs far deeper than amongst the political classes in the US or Europe. The combined impact on their economic and social prospects is not the stuff of some flaky scenario-building exercise; it's already happening right now, and the "short-term pain" is already intense.

As a potential global pace-setter on sustainability, China has three things going for it: almost limitless reserves of foreign exchange; a passion about engineering, innovation and possible technological breakthroughs; and far fewer constraints on its room for manoeuvre than is the case in any democracy. And if you look hard enough, you can already see the outline of this new economy emerging through the polluted hell-holes of the old economy, with the scale of investment that China is already directing into environmental technologies and renewable energy quite staggering. Whether that will persuade it to start taking a lead on climate change internationally is another story.

There is no historical precedent for the kind of intense international negotiations on climate change that are already underway. The Intergovernmental Panel on climate change (itself a global institution that has no

precedent and, currently, no comparator) has established
an impressively robust science base, and the UN's family
of nations now has the opportunity (through the UN
Framework Convention on Climate Change) to convert
that science into binding global agreements. As intimated
before, it may paradoxically be the sheer scale of threat
that constitutes our best hope at this stage. With growing
awareness of the potentially horrific consequences of non-
linear climate change (where the global climate flips from
one relatively stable state to a dramatically different state
in what might be a startlingly short period of time), many
now believe that it is more realistic to speculate about what
might be described as "non-linear political leadership",
with today's grudging, wholly inadequate incrementalism
'flipping' into an unprecedented manifestation of urgent,
burden-sharing solidarity, with politicians empowered by
their electorates to institute non-linear programmes of
technology shift, civic action and international cooperation.

High-level agreements of such a kind must then be
translated through into specific technology cooperation
deals so that the wave of innovation that we are just
beginning to see the first signs of becomes instantly
available to all nations, not just to those that have the
inherited intellectual capital in both Higher Education and
the private sector to build breakthrough on breakthrough.
There must of course be ways of protecting the intellectual
property embedded in those breakthroughs, but new
international financing mechanisms must clearly develop
the capability to spread those benefits as widely and as
rapidly as possible.

There is no single area where this matters more than in
the built environment. Roughly a third of energy-related
emissions of CO_2 are generated by energy used in
buildings—and experts calculate that as much as a third
of that could be eliminated by 2020 simply by deploying

existing technologies. As the Intergovernmental Panel on Climate Change pointed out in its report in May 2007, by comparison to other sectors of the economy (particularly transport, where the best available incremental gains using existing technologies will achieve little more than hold emissions constant given projected levels of growth), that 30 per cent opportunity represents a harvest of 'low-hanging fruit' of unparalleled abundance.

But the truth is, it won't pick itself. The vast majority of buildings going up in China, for instance, fail to meet what are already incredibly lax energy efficiency standards—and the current building boom shows little sign of slowing down any time soon. In March 2007, the Chinese government announced a new set of building regulations which it claimed would cut energy use in buildings by 65 per cent by 2020. But China is great at setting ambitious environmental targets, and then doing nothing at all to enforce them, and unless this particular ambition is driven all the way through the system (by incentivisation as much as by mandation), the likelihood is that China's buildings will be consuming 50 per cent more energy overall by 2020—as Mark Levine and colleagues at The Lawrence Berkeley National Laboratory in California have recently estimated. And almost all that energy will come from increased consumption of China's dirty coal.

Sadly, the situation is not that much better in the US. Part of the feel-good life for millions of Americans over the last few years has been manifested in upgrading their homes—average house size has actually doubled since 1940. Houses are now better insulated than they used to be, that's true, but the kind of rebound effect that we're seeing here (with all efficiency gains eroded away by bigger houses with more and more electrical and electronic appliances) means that energy consumption

in domestic and commercial buildings will grow at over
one per cent per annum from today through to 2030—
and that is the proud estimate of the US Department
of Energy itself, which quite perversely continues to
correlate increased energy consumption with increased
prosperity and a higher quality of life. Any suggestion
that the US might move to imitate the UK government's
bold decision to mandate zero-carbon homes by 2016 is
treated with derision by the Bush Administration.

Once again, we are straight back into the heartland of US
domestic politics. Once again, we are left contemplating
a leadership deficit that is so devastating, in both
its scale and its international impact, that it reduces
any discussion about the future of globalisation to a
discussion about the future of the US. And that is where
this enquiry must now conclude.

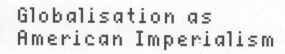

Globalisation as American Imperialism

To be part of the kind of global community referred to previously, capable of over-riding national, religious and ethnic differences in pursuit of solutions to problems faced quite literally by every single human on earth, let alone by billions of humans still to come, would be a fine and uplifting thing. One might legitimately identify in such a community of nations an upward trajectory for the human species as a whole, evidence at last of some reasonable prospect of finding ways of 'rubbing along together' perfectly adequately in the future.

But nothing could be further removed from that scenario than what we know as globalisation today. Indeed, I've felt a growing sense of ill-ease in drafting this text in that the widespread usage of the language of globalisation (as something to be admired or reviled, accelerated or transformed, but always on its own terms) may in fact be serving to obscure a far deeper, darker reality: that globalisation today is nothing more than an instrument of US policy. And just as George Bush spelled it out for the nations of the world, speaking in the National Cathedral in Washington a few days after 9/11 ("Every nation, in every region, now has a decision to make. Either you're with us, or you are with the terrorists"), there's now an increasingly clear diktat that a nation is either fully signed up to globalisation, US-style, like-it-or-not, or is just one step removed from being identified as part of the Axis of Evil.

For understandable historical reasons, the default instinct for the majority of UK citizens contemplating the role of the US in the world today is still largely positive. Even those who were and still are vigorously opposed to the Iraq War, who find George Bush both a bumbling idiot and a powerfully malign force let loose on the rest of the world, are charitably inclined to see his Administration as a temporary aberration. America is thought to have its own way of sorting out these extremes, so let's just bring back Bill Clinton, and everything will be fine. For the UK's predominantly right-wing print media, who do not see George Bush in these terms and who were all strongly in favour of the war in Iraq, America is still the nearest thing we've got to 'the land of the free, and the home of the brave', and to be its closest ally, as measured by relative amounts of blood on our hands from the continuing disaster in Iraq, is a source of considerable pride rather than intense shame. As Robert Kagan has pointed out:

It's time to stop pretending that Europeans and
Americans share a common view of the world, or even
that they occupy the same world. On major strategic and
international questions today, Americans are from Mars
and Europeans are from Venus: they agree on little and
understand one another less and less. And this state of
affairs is not transitory—the product of one American
election or one catastrophic event. The reasons for the
transatlantic divide are deep, long in development,
and likely to endure. When it comes to setting national
priorities, determining threats, defining challenges, and
fashioning and implementing foreign and defence policies,
the US and Europe have parted ways. [19]

19 Kagan, R, *Of
Paradise and
Power: America and
Europe in the New
World Order*, New
York: Alfred Knopf,
2003

Indeed, few people in the UK realise just how strange, illiberal
and divided the US has become. Wealth gaps between the
richest and the poorest get wider every year at a faster rate
than in any other country in the world. Personal debt now
exceeds $2.5 trillion; government debt exceeds $3 trillion.
Despite the fact that 50 per cent of US citizens have degrees,
only 18 per cent have a passport. Americans watch more
hours of TV every day than any other nation on Earth. There
is an almost complete lack of intelligent political discussion
outside of Washington or beyond the east and west coast
elites. America is still a deeply racially divided nation: 70
per cent of black children live below the poverty line, and
there are more blacks in jail than are in college. Electoral
success depends almost entirely on how much money you
can command, and how many favours you can call in: the
political pork-barrel is as richly endowed as it has ever been
in American history. 47 per cent of Americans describe
themselves as 'born-again' Christians, believing that the
second coming of Christ is right around the corner, and that
Darwin's Theory of Evolution is a Satanic trap specifically
designed to test believers. Working closely with these
religious fundamentalists, post 9/11, the Bush Administration
has dramatically eroded civil liberties in the US, through

the Terrorist Information Programme and the Patriot Act. Surveillance systems have been introduced in ways and places that most US citizens have no conception of, but don't seem particularly concerned about even when they do cotton on to what is actually happening.

Presiding over all this, a small but immensely influential group of neo-conservative 'fundamentalists' have taken control of many of the levers of influence and power in the US system, and have little hesitation in using them with a degree of ruthlessness that has astonished the old and, let's face it, all but emasculated liberal elite. Military budgets have been massively ramped up to succour a fully revitalised military-industrial complex, and domestic/welfare budgets have been slashed proportionately.

It is precisely that sensation of an entire nation sleepwalking into a nightmarish future that has led Theodore Roszak to speculate about a 'perfect authoritarian storm'. In "World Beware: American Triumphalism in the Age of Terror" (a book which he has not yet been able to get published in the US), Roszak undertakes a chilling dissection of those political, business and religious forces in the US that are, in effect, master-minding this gradual takeover of everything that once made America the most widely admired nation in the world:

> The leadership we need cannot come from a nation whose politics is more and more based on a social Darwinist ethic that places wealth and power above compassion and justice, a nation where the political spectrum stops at dead centre with a faint-hearted liberalism that seems uncertain that it can provide its citizens even with healthcare or pension, a nation in which the conservative party that has dominated the political scene for 20 years eagerly anticipates auctioning off the country's schools, national parks, water and power, even its armed forces, to the highest private bidder, a nation that now counts its

millionaires and billionaires in the hundreds, but where record numbers of the working poor can now be found sleeping in their cars in Wal-Mart parking lots. In short, a nation that is rapidly travelling backward towards the darkest days of free-market anarchy.[20]

20 Roszak, T, *World Beware! American Triumphalism in an Age of Terror,* Toronto: Between the Lines, 2006

So deep-seated is this malaise that Roszak is by no means persuaded that victory for the Democrats at the next election will make that much difference. Firstly, to get themselves elected, Democrats will need to stick closely to what has become an almost universalised conservatism. Whilst the majority of US citizens, for instance, may now be keen to end the war in Iraq as soon as possible, an even bigger majority is still totally committed to pursuing the 'war on terror' and apparently reconciled to the implications of the US being in a state of permanent war from herein on. Woe betide the Democrats if they dare challenge that particular consensus, however meaningless and intellectually barren it may be. And secondly, like most US progressives, Roszak believes that the Democrats long ago lost their own moral and political compass, and are not particularly uncomfortable in the kind of world the neo-conservatives and the Republican Party are fashioning under their very noses.

The implications of all this for the future of globalisation are hugely significant. The 'triumphalists' in America are intent not just on re-engineering economic and political life in the US, but on making the world over in its own image. This can be seen in its ever more ruthless manipulation of the machinery of international governance (through the World Trade Organisation, the IFC, the World Bank and so on), through its systematic hostility to the United Nations and everything it stands for, and through its rejection of a host of key treaties and international agreements.

Two new books will serve to bring it home to well-meaning European liberals just how deeply disturbing the shift in

America has been over the last couple of decades. Naomi Klein's *The Shock Doctrine; the Rise of Disaster Capitalism* sets out unapologetically to jolt readers into understanding how a tiny elite of neo-conservative fundamentalists (both political, as disciples of Milton Friedman, and religious) have commandeered capital markets, the media and a complacent, lazy population to secure an unprecedented power base. Rather more surprisingly, Al Gore's *An Assault on Reason* is a passionate and utterly compelling attack on President Bush and on the way he has set out to subvert and threaten the very integrity of the US Constitution:

> Respect for our President is important. But even more important is respect for our Constitution... democracy itself is in danger if we allow any president to use his role as Commander-in-Chief to rupture the careful balance between the executive, legislative and judicial branches of government.... President Bush has determinedly conflated his role of Commander-in-Chief with his roles of Head of Government and Head of State, and in so doing, he has maximised the power he has been given by Americans who are fearful of being attacked and are eager to receive his promises of protection... the survival of freedom depends upon the rule of law... President Bush has repeatedly violated the law for six years... the consequences to our democracy of silently ignoring serious and repeated violations to the law by the President of the US are extremely serious.[21]

21 Gore, A,
The Assault on Reason, London: Bloomsbury, 2007

The idea of reforming globalisation (as in the kind of model recommended by Joseph Stiglitz in *Making Globalisation Work*) let alone transforming it, against that kind of unapologetically self-serving, unilateralist US hegemony, is frankly naïve. On every single 'big ticket' opportunity for harnessing the power of globalisation to help address today's most pressing global challenges, the US is pulling in the wrong direction. The Oxford Research Group, in its 2007 report on *Global Responses to*

Global Threats, demonstrates how the US-led global agenda has adopted a 'control paradigm' essentially to try and keep the lid on things and to maintain a status quo that continues to work so powerfully in the interests of the world's elites. It contrasts this with what it calls a 'sustainable security paradigm':

> The main difference between this and the 'control paradigm' is that this approach does not attempt to unilaterally control threats through the use of force ('attack the symptoms'), but rather it aims to cooperatively resolve the root causes of those threats using the most effective means available ('cure the disease'). Furthermore, a sustainable security approach is inherently preventative, in that it addresses the likely causes of conflict and instability well before the ill-effects are felt, rather than waiting until the crisis is underway and then attempting to control the situation, at which point it is often too late. It follows that this cooperative approach must be coordinated through a reformed United Nations, as individual governments or 'coalitions' are too focused on their own interests.[22]

22 Abbott, C, P, Rogers and J, Sloboda, *Global Responses to Global Threats: Sustainable Security for the 21st Century*, Oxford: The Oxford Research Group, 2006

In terms of the five most pressing global threats, that humankind now faces, that produces the following comparison:

The simple conclusion arising out of insights of this kind is that there will be no planned, managed transition to a more benign form of globalisation unless and until 'the rogue nation' that the US has become is itself brought back into the Family of Nations.

This places a very special onus on the UK, commensurate with its own sense of a 'special' relationship with the US. Tony Blair's disgraceful complicity in legitimising the illegal war in Iraq (and it's as well not to forget too quickly the contribution that his wholly dishonest warnings about weapons of mass destruction and "missiles ready to launch in 45 minutes"

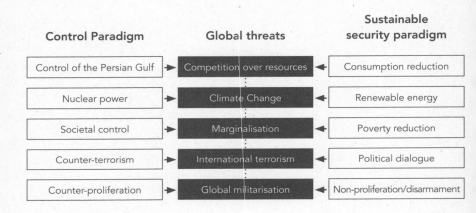

Control Paradigm	Global threats	Sustainable security paradigm
Control of the Persian Gulf	Competition over resources	Consumption reduction
Nuclear power	Climate Change	Renewable energy
Societal control	Marginalisation	Poverty reduction
Counter-terrorism	International terrorism	Political dialogue
Counter-proliferation	Global militarisation	Non-proliferation/disarmament

made to winning over so many other nations—let alone
his own reluctant party—to go along with the withdrawal
of UN weapons inspectors as a precursor to the war itself)
means we now have little moral standing as far as the
rest of the world is concerned. It is by no means certain
that it has given the UK any additional leverage in the
US either, and the callous insouciance with which George
Bush refused to make even the smallest concession
to Tony Blair on the G8 Climate Change negotiations
demonstrates the utter folly of supposing that one can
do 'special deals' with an Administration dominated by
the likes of George Bush, Dick Cheney and other neo-
conservative zealots.

Whatever else Gordon Brown may now do in terms of
redefining that 'special relationship', the starting point
articulated by Mark Malloch Brown (Junior Minister at
the Foreign and Commonwealth Office) of asserting that
the UK and the US will "no longer be joined at the hip",
as they were under Tony Blair's leadership, is certainly an
encouraging one.

Civic Globalisation

In terms of the competing models of globalisation outlined in "Global Futures", I hope it has become increasingly clear that the future of regionalism (as in vibrant, culturally and politically diverse, ecologically coherent spatial entities, capable of generating a high material standard of living within its respective social and environmental carrying capacities) depends utterly on which particular model of globalisation you think will prevail. US-led, corporatist globalisation remains implacably hostile to the re-emergence of strong, self-reliant regions; what might be described as "civic globalisation" will not only nurture that kind of regionalism, but depend for its own success upon it. Wolfgang Sachs captures the dichotomy as follows:

Market-driven globalisation is interested in turning the whole world into a single economic space; transnationally active corporations are supposed to compete globally with one another, to increase wealth and prosperity in the world as efficiently as possible. On the other side, the conception of a politically-driven globalisation sees the world not as an economic arena but as a community in which people, nations and societies co-exist with one another; this community should develop institutions committed to the common good, and that requires constant weighing of the values of democracy, ecology and economic utility. To sum up the difference, we may say that advocates of politically driven globalisation look at the world and see a society that has a market, whereas advocates of market-driven globalisation look at the world and see a society that is a market.[23]

23 Sachs, *Fair Future*

It is in the nature of today's polarised debate about globalisation that this alternative model of "civic globalisation" invariably gets ignored. So keen are campaigners to warn society of the dangers of corporatist globalisation that almost all their available energy goes into demolition rather than constructive visioning. But by any set of insights into the dominant physical and political realities of the next 20 years (as mapped out in "2025—For better or for worse"), the likelihood of today's model of corporatist globalisation managing to weather the storms ahead, protected though it may currently be by heavyweight institutions like the WTO, the World Bank and the IFC, let alone by the power of the US imperium, would appear to me to be negligible. A less "future-proofed" political edifice it is difficult to imagine.

Civic globalisation must therefore be seen as a critical part of the "breakthrough" process that could (I do not dare say "will"!) emerge out of an almost inevitable period of traumatic breakdown ahead of us. For the idealists who see history as a process of slow but steady integration between potentially conflicted peoples, moving over many millennia from warring tribal entities to the point where we now have a better sense of ourselves as one than ever before, that is really what true, non-economic globalisation has always promised. Some commentators have drawn the analogy here between those theories of child development which see children moving away from absolute egocentricity to increasingly empathetic relationships with other people, and a comparable path of evolutionary development for humankind as a species. Seen through the lens of this "glass more than half full" perspective, those key attributes of loyalty and trust, which in part make us the species we are, are being gradually extended from family through to community through to nation state through, perhaps, to becoming a world society.

And the paradox, as I have said before, is that it's precisely the scale and mind-numbing potential severity of global environmental shocks such as climate change.

Appendix: Forum for the Future's 'Working Vision' of a Sustainable Future

We all want the best possible schools and hospitals, the safest streets, the highest physical quality of life, and the fairest and most effective democratic processes, and we will go on seeking them just as keenly in a sustainable society as we do today. The likelihood that things will, in all probability, be more decentralised, with a lot more going on at the human scale and the community level, won't actually change any of that.

Some of the economics will not be all that different either: fair prices in properly regulated markets; efficient and reliable public services; a commitment to ensure access to job opportunities and fulfilling work; and so on. No hair-shirt asceticism, but far less frenetic consumerism, less shopping for the sake of shopping, less conspicuous consumption, less waste, less keeping up with the Joneses—with more time, therefore, to do more of the things that people today always claim to regret not having the time to do.

There will also be a lot less international trade. A watchword of sustainable economics is self-reliance. This entails combining judicious and necessary trade with other countries with an unapologetic emphasis on each country maintaining security of supply in terms of energy, food and even manufacturing. The idea that today's neo-liberal, no-holds-barred model of globalisation will last much longer seems fantastical anyway, as nation after nation feels the pain of China and other lowest-cost economies making it all but impossible to compete in any serious sense.

With oil trading at well over $100 dollars a barrel, some of the most absurd anomalies of international trade and travel (apples from New Zealand, £10 flights to dozens of destinations, and so on) will have long since disappeared. As part of our efforts to mitigate the worst threats of climate change, each individual will have his/her own carbon quota, allocated on an annual basis, and finding ways of living elegant, low-carbon lives will be both fashionable and profitable. This should usher in the first moment in modern history where cyclists have the edge on the owners of the next generation of gas-guzzling SUVs!

And there is no point beating around the bush on one other thing: people who are better off will almost certainly be paying higher taxes than they do today. Two of the cornerstones of a sustainable economy are increased efficiency (in terms of resources, energy, raw materials, value for money, capital allocation and so on) and social justice. No serious definition of the word 'sustainable' could possibly allow for a continuation of the grotesque disparities in wealth that we see today, both within countries and between countries.

Suggested Reading

General

"Barker Review of Land Use Planning", Department of Communities and Local Government, 2006.

Florida, Richard, *The Rise of the Creative Class*, London: Basic Books, 2002.

Foxell Simon, ed., *The professionals' choice: The future of the built environment professions*, London: Building Futures, 2003.

Kunstler, James Howard, *The Long Emergency*, Atlantic Monthly Press, 2005.

Leadbeater, Charles, *Personalisation through participation: A new script for public services*, London: Demos, 2004.

Schumacher, EF, *Small is Beautiful*, Vancouver: Hartley & Marks,1999.

Economic Survey of the United Kingdom, OECD, 2007.

World Population Prospects: The 2006 Revision, Population Division of the Department of Economic and Social Affairs of the United Nations Secretariat, United Nations, 2007.

Planet Earth and Climate Change

Flannery, Tim, *The Weather Makers: The History and Future Impact of Climate Change*, Melbourne: Text Publishing, 2005.

Gore, Al, *Earth in the Balance: Ecology and the Human Spirit*, Boston: Houghton Mifflin, 1992.

Gore, Al, *The Assault on Reason*, Harmondsworth: Penguin, 2007.

Hartmann, Thom, *Last Hours of Ancient Sunlight*, New York: Three Rivers Press, 1997 (rev. 2004).

Hawken, Lovins & Lovins, *Natural Capitalism*, London: Little Brown, 1999.

Hillman, Mayer, *How We Can Save the Planet*, Harmondsworth: Penguin, 2004.

Homer-Dixon, Thomas, *The Upside of Down: Catastrophe, Creativity and the Renewal of Civilisation*, New York: Alfred A Knopf, 2006.

Kolbert, Elizabeth, *Field Notes from a Catastrophe: A Frontline Report on Climate Change*, London: Bloomsbury, 2006.

Lovelock, James, *Gaia: A New Look at Life on Earth*, Oxford: Oxford University Press, 1979.

Lovelock, James, *The Revenge of Gaia*, London: Allen Lane, 2006.

Lynas, Mark, *High Tide: The Truth About Our Climate Crisis*, London: Picador, 2004.

Lynas, Mark, *Six Degrees: Our Future on a Hotter Planet*, London: Fourth Estate, 2007.

Marshall, George, *Carbon Detox*, London: Gaia Thinking, 2007.

McDonough, W, and Braungert M, *Cradle to Cradle, Remaking the Way We Make Things*, New York: North Point Press, 2002.

Monbiot, George, *Heat: How We Can Stop the Planet Burning*, London: Allen Lane, 2006.

Walker, G, and King D, *The Hot Topic: How to Tackle Global Warming and Still Keep the Lights On*, London: Bloomsbury, 2008.

Action Today to Protect Tomorrow—The Mayor's Climate Change Action Plan, London: GLA, 2007.

Climate Change The UK Programme, London: DEFRA, 2006.

Summary for Policymakers of the Synthesis Report of the IPCC Fourth Assessment Report, United Nations, 2007.

Cities

Girardet, Herbert, *Cities People Planet: Liveable Cities for a Sustainable World*, Chichester: Wiley-Academy, 2004.

Jacobs, Jane, *The Death and Life of Great American Cities*, New York: Random House, 1961.

Jacobs, Jane, *The Economy of Cities*, New York: Random House, 1969.

Mumford, Lewis, *The Culture of Cities*, New York: Secker & Warburg, 1938.

Sudjic, Deyan, "Cities on the edge of chaos", *The Observer*, March 2008.

Urban Task Force, *Towards an Urban Renaissance*, London: E&FN Spon, 1999.

Work

Abramson, Daniel M, *Building the Bank of England*, New Haven, CT: Yale University Press, 2005.

Alexander, Christopher, *The Timeless Way of Building*, Oxford: Oxford University Press, 1979.

Anderson, Ray, *Mid-Course Correction: The Interface Model*, Chelsea Green, 2007.

Brand, Stewart, *How Buildings Learn*, New York: Viking Press, 1994.

Brinkley, Ian, *Defining the Knowledge Economy*, Knowledge Economy Programme Report, London: The Work Foundation, 2006.

Castells, Manuel, *The Information Age: Economy, Society, Culture*, Oxford: Blackwell, 1996.

Davenport, Tom, *Thinking for a Living*, Boston: Harvard Business School Press, 2005.

Dodgson, Gann, and Salter, *Think, Play, Do*, Oxford, 2005.

Dodgson, Gann and Salter, *The management of technological innovation strategy and practice*, Oxford: Oxford University Press, 2008.

Duffy, Francis, *The Changing Workplace*, London: Phaidon, 1992.

Duffy, Francis, *The New Office*, London: Conran Octopus, 1997.

Duffy, Francis, *Architectural Knowledge*, London: E&FN Spon, 1998.

Duffy, Cave, Worthington, *Planning Office Space*, London: The Architectural Press, 1976.

Galloway, L, *Office Management: Its Principles and Practice*, Oxford: The Ronald Press, 1918.

Gann, David, *Building Innovation*, London: Thomas Telford, 2000.

Giedion, Siegfried, *Mechanization Takes Command*, Oxford: Oxford University Press, 1948.

Gilbreth, FB, *Motion Study*, New York: Van Nostrand, 1911.

Gottfried, David, *Greed to Green*, Berkeley, CA: Worldbuild Publishing, 2004.

Groak, Steven, *Is Construction an Industry?*, Construction Management and Economics, 1994.

Handy, Charles, *Understanding Organizations*, Harmondsworth: Penguin, 1967.

Hawken, Paul, *The Ecology of Commerce*, New York: HarperCollins, 1993.

Mitchell, William J, *City of Bits*, Cambridge, MA: MIT Press, 1995.

Quinan, Jack, *Frank Lloyd Wright's Larkin Building*, Cambridge, MA: MIT Press, 1987.

Sassen, Saskia, *A Sociology of Globalization*, New York: Norton, 2006.

Sennett, Richard, *The Culture of the New Capitalism*, New Haven, CT: Yale University Press, 2006.

Taylor, Frederick, *The Principles of Scientific Management*, New York: Harper & Brothers, 1911.

Trease, Geoffrey, *Samuel Pepys and His World*, London: Thames and Hudson, 1972.

Education

Aston and Bekhradnia, *Demand for Graduates: A review of the economic evidence*, Higher Education Policy Institute, 2003.

Friere, Paolo, *Education: the practice of freedom*, London: Writers and Readers Cooperative, 1974.

Gardner, Howard, *Multiple Intelligences*, New York: Basic Books, 1993.

Goodman, Paul,
Growing up absurd,
New York: First Sphere Books,
1970.

Illich, Ivan, *Deschooling
Society*, London: Calder and
Boyars.1971.

Kimber, Mike, Does
Size Matter? *Distributed
leadership in small secondary
schools*, National College for
School Leadership, 2003.

Nair and Fielding, *The
Language of School Design*,
DesignShare, 2005.

Neil, AS, Summerhill,
Harmondsworth: Penguin
Books,1968.
*The Children's Plan—Building
Brighter Futures*, DCSF,
December 2007.

*Every Child Matters: Change
for Children*, DfES/HM
Government, 2004.

*Higher Standards, Better
Schools For All*, DfES.

*2020 Vision Report of the
Teaching and Learning in
2020*, Review Group, 2006.

www.smallschools.org.uk

www.thecademy.net/
inclusiontrust.org/
Welcome.html

www.eco-schools.org.uk

www.standards.dfes.gov.uk/
personalisedlearning/about/

Transport and Neighbourhoods

Banister, David,
*Unsustainable Transport:
City Transport in the New
Century*, London: E&FN
Spon, 2005.

Bertolini L, and T, Spit, *Cities
on Rails. The Redevelopment
of Railway Station Areas*,
London: Spon/Routledge,
1998.

Calthorpe P, and Fulton, W,
*The Regional City: Planning
for the End of Sprawl*,
Washington, DC: Island
Press, 2003.

Dittmar H, and Ohland, G,
*The New Transit Town:
Best Practices in Transit-
Oriented Development*,
Washington, DC: Island
Press, 2004.

Hickman, R and Banister, D,
*Looking over the horizon,
Transport and reduced CO_2
emissions in the UK by 2030*,
Transport Policy, 2007.

Holtzclaw, Clear, Dittmar, Goldstein and Haas, *Location Efficiency: Neighborhood and Socioeconomic Characteristics Determine Auto Ownership and Use*, Transportation Planning and Technology (Vol. 25) 2002.

Commission for Integrated Transport, Planning for High Speed Rail Needed Now, 2004, viewed at http://www.cfit.gov.uk/pn/040209/index.htm

Regional Transport Statistics, National Statistics and Department for Transport, 2006 Edition.

Energy, Transport and Environment Indicators, Eurostat, 2005 Edition.

Toward a Sustainable Transport system, Department for Transport, 2007.

Eddington Transport Study, HM Treasury & Department for Transport, 2007.

UK Foresight programme, *Tackling Obesities: Future Choices*, The Government Office for Science and Technology, 2007.

Community

Dench G, Gavron K, and Young M, *The New East End: Kinship*, Race and Conflict, London: Profile, 2006.

Jacobs, Jane, *The Death and Life of American Cities*, New York: Modern Library, 1961.

Putnam, Robert, *Bowling Alone: The Collapse and Revival of American Community*, New York: Simon & Schuster, 2000.

Young M, and Willmott, P, *Family and Kinship in East London*, Harmondsworth: Penguin, 1957.

Report Card 7, *Child poverty in perspective: An overview of child well-being in rich countries*, UNICEF Innocenti Research Centre, 2007.

Key Facts for Diverse Communities: Ethnicity and Faith, Greater London Authority, Data Management and Analysis Group, 2007.

www.footprintnetwork.org

www.yourhistoryhere

www.fixmystreet.com

Globalisation

Abbott, C, Rogers, P, Sloboda, J, *Global Responses to Global Threats: Sustainable Security for the 21st Century*, Oxford: The Oxford Research Group, 2006.

Balls E, Healey J and Leslie C, *Evolution and Devolution in England*, New Local Government Network, 2006.

Gladwell, Malcolm, *The Tipping Point: How Little Things Can Make a Big Difference*, London: Little Brown, 2000.

Goldsmith, Edward, "How to Feed People under a Regime of Climate Change", *Ecologist Magazine*, 2004.

Gore, Al, *The Assault on Reason*, London: Bloomsbury, 2007.

Gray, John, *Black Mass: Apocalyptic Religion and the Death of Utopia*, London: Allen Lane, 2007.

Guillebaud, John, Youthquake: *Population, Fertility and Environment in the 21st Century*, Optimum Population Trust, 2007.

Hines, Colin, *Localisation: A Global Manifesto*, London: Earthscan, 2000.

Kagan, Robert, *Of Paradise and Power: America and Europe in the New World Order*, New York: Alfred Knopf, 2003.

Martin, James, *The Meaning of the 21st Century*, London: Transworld, 2007.

Meadows, Meadows, Randers and Behrens, *Limits to Growth*, Club of Rome, 1972.

Nordhaus, T, and M, Shellenberger, *Break Through: From the Death of Environmentalism to the Politics of Possibility*, Boston: Houghton Mifflin, 2007.

Porritt, Jonathon, *Capitalism: As if the World Matters*, London: Earthscan, 2005.

Roszak, Theodore, *World Beware! American Triumphalism in an Age of Terror*, Toronto: Between the Lines, 2006.

Sachs, W, and T, Santarius *Fair Future: Resource Conflicts, Security and Global Justice*, London: Zed Books, 2005.

Kirkpatrick Sale, *Dwellers in the Land*, New Society Publishers, 1991.

Shrybman, Steven, *A Citizen's Guide to the World Trade Organisation*, Ottawa, Canadian Center for Policy Alternatives, 1999.

Soros, George, *The Age of Fallability: The Consequences of the War on Terror*, Beverly Hills, CA: Phoenix Books, 2006.

Stern, Nicholas, *The Economics of Climate Change: The Stern Review*, Cambridge: Cambridge University Press, 2007.

Stiglitz, Joseph, *Globalization and its Discontents*, New York: Norton, 2002.

Stiglitz, Joseph, *Making Globalization Work*, New York: Norton, 2006.

Wolf, Martin, *Why Globalization Works*, New Haven, CT: Yale University Press, 2005.

Johannesburg Manifesto, Fairness in a Fragile World, Berlin: Heinrich Böll Foundation, 2002.

US Defence Dept, *An Abrupt Climate Change Scenario and It's Implications for US Natural Security*, 2003.

WWF, Living Planet Report, WWF International, 2006.

Further websites

The Edge
www.at-the-edge.org.uk

CABE
www.cabe.org.uk

China Dialogue
www.chinadialogue.net

Global Commons Institute (Contraction and Convergence)
www.gci.org.uk

Authors

Chris Twinn
Chris Twinn is a Senior Partner at the global consulting firm Arup and is director of their sustainable buildings team.

Jonathon Porritt
Jonathon Porritt is a Co-Founder and Programme Director of Forum for the Future and is a highly respected writer, broadcaster and commentator on sustainable development. He was appointed Chairman of the UK Sustainable Development Commission in July 2000 and was formerly Director of Friends of the Earth, 1984–1990 and a co-chair of the Green Party, 1980–1983, of which he is still a member. His latest book, *Capitalism as if the World Matters*, was published in November 2005.

The Edge

The Edge is a ginger group and think tank, sponsored by the
building industry professions, that seeks to stimulate public interest
in policy questions that affect the built environment, and to inform
and influence public opinion. It was established in 1996 with
support from the Arup Foundation. The Edge is supported by
The Carbon Trust.

The Edge organises a regular series of debates and other events
intended to advance policy thinking in the built environment sector
and among the professional bodies within it. For further details, see
www.at-the-edge.org.uk

Edge Futures

Edge Futures is a project initiated by The Edge and Black Dog Publishing. It has only been possible with the active participation of The Edge Committee as well as supporting firms and institutions. Special thanks are due to Adam Poole, Duncan McCorquodale, Frank Duffy, Robin Nicholson, Bill Gething, Chris Twinn, Andy Ford, Mike Murray and Jane Powell as well as to all the individual authors.

The project has been generously sponsored by The Carbon Trust, The Commission for Architecture and the Built Environment (CABE), Ramboll Whitbybird, The Arup Foundation, ProLogis and Construction Skills. Thanks are due to all those bodies and to the support of Karen Germain, Elanor Warwick, Mark Whitby, Ken Hall and Guy Hazlehurst within them.
The Edge is also grateful to Sebastian Macmillan of IDBE in Cambridge for the day we spent developing scenarios there and to Philip Guildford for facilitating the session.

Simon Foxell

Much is already known about the state of the
world 15 to 20 years from now. Almost all the
buildings and infrastructure are already in place
or in development—we replace our buildings
etc., at a very slow pace. The great majority of
the population who'll be living and working then,
especially in the UK, have already been born and
will have been educated in a school system that is
familiar and predictable. The global population,
however, will have increased from 6.7 billion in
July 2007 to approximately 8 billion by 2025.

The climate will have changed, mainly as a result of
the emissions of greenhouse gases of the past 50
and more years, but not by much. The temperature
is predicted to be, on average, half a degree
warmer, as well as varying over a greater range than
at present. But, more significantly it will be
understood to be changing, resulting in a strong
feeling of uncertainty and insecurity. Rainfall will have
reduced but will also become more extreme, i.e.
tending to drought or flood. Resources, whether
energy, water or food imports, will be in shorter
supply; partly as a result of climate change but also
due to regulations aimed at preventing the effects of
global warming becoming worse. Transport will be
constrained as a result but other technologies will
have greatly improved the ability to economically
communicate.

These changes form the context for this first
series of five Edge Futures books, but it is not
their subject: that is the impact of such changes
and other developments on our daily lives, the
economy, social and education services and the
way the world trades and operates. Decision
makers are already being challenged to act and

formulate policy, in the face of the change already apparent in the years ahead. This set of books highlights how critical and important planning for the future is going to be. Society will expect and require policy makers to have thought ahead and prepared for the best as well as the worst. Edge Futures offers a series of critical views of events, in the next two decades, that need to be planned for today.

The five books intentionally look at the future from very different viewpoints and perspectives. Each author, or pair of authors, has been asked to address a different sector of society, but there is inevitably a great deal of crossover between them. They do not always agree; but consistency is not the intention; that is to capture a breadth of vision as where we may be in 20 years time.

Jonathon Porritt in *Globalism and Regionalism* examines some of the greatest challenges before the planet, including climate change and demographic growth, and lays down the gauntlet to the authors of the other books. Porritt's diagnosis of the need to establish a new balance between the global and the regional over the years ahead and to achieve a 'Civic Globalisation' has an echo in Geoff Mulgan's call in *Living and Community* for strengthening communities through rethinking local governance and rebuilding a sense of place. Both are—perhaps professionally—optimistic that the climate change is a challenge that we, as a society, can deal with, while not underestimating the change that our society is going to have to undergo to achieve it.

Hank Dittmar, writing in *Transport and Networks* is less than certain, that currently, policies are adequately joined-up to deal with the issues

that the recent flurry of major reports from the
UK Government has highlighted: "Planning"
from Barker, "Climate Change" from Stern and
"Transport" from Eddington. He notes Barker's
comment that "planning plays a role in the
mitigation of and adaptation to climate change,
the biggest issue faced across all climate areas"but
that she then goes on to dismiss the issue. In its
approach to all these reviews, the government has
shown that it is more concerned with economic
growth and indeed it has already concluded that
the transport network needs no further fundamental
reform. Dittmar believes otherwise, he calls for
immediate solutions to support the development of
the accessible, sustainable city.

Simon Foxell in *Education and Creativity* sees an
even bumpier ride ahead, with progress only being
made as a result of the lurch from crisis to crisis. Such
discontinuities, will allow the UK to address many
longstanding problems, from the personalisation of
education to addressing the increasingly cut-throat
international competition in creativity, innovation
and skills—but not without a great deal of pain and
chaos. Bill Mitchell, in the same volume, outlines
a way of reconfiguring educational practice to
develop just those skills that successful creativity-
based economies are going to require.

In *Working*, Frank Duffy sees the end of road
for the classic 'American Taylorist' office and the
unsuitability of its counterpart, the European social
democratic office. In their place, he proposes a
new typology—the networked office—that will
make better use of the precious resource that is
our existing stock of buildings and allow greater
integration into the life of the city. And, it is the

city that all the authors come back to as a central and unifying theme—the dominant form of the millennium, the place where the majority of mankind now lives. Perhaps this is because, as Deyan Sudjic, Director of the Design Museum, has written recently; "The future of the city has suddenly become the only subject in town."

It is about the largest social unit that most of us can imagine with any ease and is a constant challenge economically, socially and environmentally. If we can work out what a sustainable city might be like and how to deliver it, then maybe we can sleep easier in our beds, less afraid that the end of civilisation, as we recognise it, may be within our childrens', or our childrens' childrens', lifetime. All the component parts of the Edge Futures studies come together in the city; where the community meets the office buildings, the schools and transport system. The city is the hub of the regional response to world events and needs to become a responsive participant in formulating a way out of policy log-jam.

As this first series of Edge Futures shows, the task is urgent and deeply complex but also not impossible. It is only, assuming that we need to make the transition to a low carbon economy within ten to twenty years, in Geoff Mulgan's words: "extraordinarily challenging by any historic precedent."

10a Acton Street
London WC1X 9NG
T. +44 (0)20 7613 1922
F. +44 (0)20 7613 1944
E. info@blackdogonline.com
W. www.blackdogonline.com

Designed by Draught Associates

All opinions expressed within this publication are those of the authors and
not necessarily of the publisher.

British Library Cataloguing-in-Publication Data.
A CIP record for this book is available from the British Library.
ISBN: 978 1 906155 148

Black Dog Publishing, London, UK is an environmentally responsible
company. Edge Futures are printed on Cyclus Offset, a paper produced
from 100% post consumer waste.

architecture art design
fashion history photography
theory and things

www.blackdogonline.com